LANCASHIRE'S FORGOTTEN
HEROES

8th (Service) Battalion, East Lancashire Regiment in the Great War

STEPHEN BARKER AND CHRISTOPHER BOARDMAN

Press

This book is dedicated to all those who fought with the 8th Battalion of the East Lancashire Regiment 1914–18, including our family members: 16316 Company Sergeant-Major James Fleming MC, DCM and 17378 Lance-Sergeant John Barker.

First published 2008

The History Press
The Mill, Brimscombe Port
Stroud, Gloucestershire, GL5 2QG
www.thehistorypress.co.uk

© Stephen Barker and Christopher Boardman, 2008

The right of Stephen Barker and Christopher Boardman
to be identified as the Authors
of this work has been asserted in accordance with the
Copyrights, Designs and Patents Act 1988.

British Library Cataloguing in Publication Data.
A catalogue record for this book is available from the British Library.

ISBN 978 0 7524 4812 1

Typesetting and origination by The History Press
Printed in Great Britain

CONTENTS

ACKNOWLEDGEMENTS

During the planning and writing of this book over the last two years, an ever-increasing number of individuals have become involved in the process. Some did so consciously, others unwittingly, without realising into what they were being drawn! To all who have supported us, we are both immensely grateful.

We would like to thank Dr Bill Mitchinson for the generous foreword and for reading all the proofs before publication. Bill's encouragement, wise counsel and knowledge of the First World War have been invaluable.

Thanks are due to Amy Rigg at The History Press for seeing merit in the material at an early stage, and also to Philip Boardman for maintaining the 'galloping 8th' website, taking photographs abroad and carrying out many other supporting roles too numerous to mention. We are indebted to Alan Sargeant for helping to provide the best possible images, many of which were from ninety-year-old newspapers.

We owe a good deal to Martin Marix-Evans for his advice and support at the planning stage, not to mention his great kindness in allowing access to his collection of written and photographic material, and also to Denis Otter for the generous and public-spirited way in which he has permitted access to his collection of obituaries of men from the Burnley area. Thank you to Andrea Burlingham for proofreading the text, drawing some of the maps and offering sage advice throughout.

Christopher and I are particularly appreciative of the following individuals and organisations that have permitted access to and use of their collections and given invaluable assistance: Yvonne Oliver and Tom Eaton at the Imperial War Museum, London; Lieutenant-Colonel John Downham MBE and Jane Davies at Fulwood Barracks Museum, Preston; Richard Davies at the Liddle Collection, Leeds University; Brenda Goldberg at the Jewish Military Museum, London; David Fletcher at the Tank Museum, Bovington; Ian Hook at the Essex Regiment Museum, Chelmsford; Steve Bull at the Museum of Lancashire, Preston; Keith Burrows and Catherine Duckworth at Accrington Local Studies Library; Diana Rishton at the Community History Collection of Blackburn with Darwen Library and Information Service; Susan Halstead at Lancashire County Library and Information Service, Burnley Library; Catherine Smythe at the Rossendale Free Press; Wendy Lord at the Bacup Museum; Ian Savage at the *Bury Times*; Margaret Parsons at the *Burnley Express* and Lyn Ashwell at the *Bolton News*.

We have been very appreciative of and moved by the individuals who have permitted us to use significant material relating to family members who had served with the battalion. All of the following have been very generous in the giving of their time, thoughts and the right to use their family archives: Tom Yuille in Northwood, as regards his father Lieutenant Archibald Yuille; Ian Darlington in New York City, concerning his great uncle Private Harold Darlington; Anthony Fleischer in Cape Town, with reference to his father Lieutenant Spencer Fleischer; Joe Heap in Colne, concerning his father Private Thomas Heap; Peter Wakefield in Anderton, as regards his grandfather Private Peter Wakefield and Amanda Skipworth in London and her family, relating to her great-grandfather Private Alfred Skipworth.

We have also been thankful for the support of the following individuals who have offered us help and advice of various kinds: John Kliene, John Dyer, Terry Crawford, Jacob Barker, Pam and Ken Linge, Ken Stone, Anne and Ian Fraser, Gary Smith, Paul Blackhurst, David Hough, Peter Wood, Joe Hodgson, Bryan and Carol Fahey, Pierre Tesserine, Steve Bury, Andrew Gill, Paul Bailie, Dave Ingham, Peter Cunliffe, Shirley Leeming, Lorraine English, Romy Wyeth, Philip Robbins, Roger Lowrie, Chris Travers at Collins & Darwell Printers and Malte Znaniecki for access to his collection of images at www.flanderland.de and www.1914–18.info.

If all else failed, we knew that the members of the civilised First World War forum (http://1914–1918.invisionzone.com) would have an answer. Many thanks go to all those who contributed, and whose collective knowledge and kindness are unsurpassed.

Very special thanks go to our parents David and June Barker, and Albert and Eileen Boardman. Thanks also to Kathleen Fleming and all other members of the Fleming and Barker families who have played a part over the years.

Last but not least, we owe a debt of gratitude to our wives Andi and Julie for their unceasing patience and support. Mention should also be made of our children Jacob, Bethany, William and Curtis, who from time to time unsuspectingly accompanied their dads on the trail of the 8th East Lancashire. It is our hope that war does not come to them as it did their forebears.

In spite of the guidance and assistance that we have received, we accept that any errors made in the book are our own. Every effort has been made to trace the copyright holders of illustrations used. Where it has not been established the authors would be grateful to anyone who believes that they do hold such a copyright to get in touch with the publishers.

Words marked with an asterisk in the text are to be found in the Glossary.

Stephen Barker and Christopher Boardman
February 2008

FOREWORD

The 8th (Service) Battalion, East Lancashire Regiment was, in some ways, an unremarkable unit of the British Expeditionary Force. It was raised as a K3 Battalion at Preston in September 1914 and, like many other Kitchener units, spent the first twenty-two months of its existence struggling for clothing and equipment in various training areas in Southern England. Although raised at the same times as the 'Pals' movement swept the country, the 8th Battalion was not one of those flamboyant creations. Instead, it was one that required men not only from different parts of Lancashire but also from several different regiments to establish it. It was initially allocated to 74 Brigade of the 25th Division, but then spent three months as Army Troops before finally being posted to 112 Brigade, 37th Division.

Like the battalion, the 37th Division was, at first glance, very ordinary. Technically, it was a K5 formation but it had been largely cobbled together from K1, K2 and K3 Battalions, most of which had themselves also been attached as Army Troops to a variety of New Army Divisions. The new division enjoyed no territorial designation, its battalions being drawn from areas as far apart as Bedfordshire, Warwickshire and Lancashire. Its only vaguely homogenous brigade, composed of four battalions of the Leicestershire Regiment, was taken from it soon after it arrived in France and was exchanged for a brigade that included one nominally regular battalion of the Middlesex Regiment and three service battalions raised respectively in Lincolnshire, Somerset and South Yorkshire. Nevertheless, the division took part in some of the fiercest engagements on the Western Front. It fought on the Somme, at Arras, in six separate battles in the sloughs before Ypres and, by the end of the war, no fewer than five of its battalions had been disbanded. The fatality roll of the 8th East Lancs itself had reached almost 600, a fairly typical figure for a New Army unit.

In recent years, local and military historians have tended to concentrate on recording the stories of the major Pals units raised by the Corporations of Leeds, Manchester, Birmingham and Tyneside, as well as those recruited by individual towns. Although this work has added substantially to our understanding of this very British wartime phenomenon, it has meant that many of the less well-known battalions of the New Armies have been largely ignored. There have been studies of some of the early Kitchener units but, at present, this work is at best patchy. To add to our knowledge and to remember and commemorate the experiences of the men of those units, Stephen Barker and Christopher Boardman have constructed a very readable and fascinating account of this little-known battalion. The two authors have trawled local and national sources extensively to build a picture, not of a unit belonging to one of the more successful of the Kitchener divisions, but of one that, although rarely attracting plaudits, was recognised as dependable and reliable. It was a battalion that by sheer hard work and dogged perseverance sometimes achieved its objectives. On other occasions, ferocious enemy resistance, a lack of effective artillery co-ordination or simply the trenchant combination of adverse weather and terrain conspired to prevent it from securing anything other than additions to its steadily mounting casualty list.

Through an examination of personal diaries, newspapers obituaries, a varied selection of photographs, many of which have never before been published, and a comprehensive range of secondary sources, the story and character of this battalion has been told. It is an account of fortitude, endeavour and duty, but one that also contains a slightly ironic twist. When, in January 1918, the Army Council decided that it no longer required the services of the 8th East Lancashire, the unit was disbanded and over 400 of its men were despatched to the regiment's 11th Battalion. Although it enjoyed a lower seniority than the 8th, it had a more emotive and familiar title. The few surviving originals of the 8th Battalion were now to become members of the 'Accrington Pals'.

Dr Bill Mitchinson
Centre for First World War Studies
University of Birmingham

INTRODUCTION

In 1994, the Vicar of St Bartholomew's in Colne opened a bin bag in the church cellar and found that it contained the colour of a British Army Regiment. As the fabric was in very poor condition, he brought it to the attention of the local Royal British Legion Club. Its members subsequently spent £1,500 having the colour restored and the following year, in the presence of various dignitaries, it was remounted at St Bartholomew's. It was the King's Colour of the 8th (Service) Battalion of the East Lancashire Regiment during 1914–18.

The 90th anniversaries of the last year of the First World War will pass by this year. That conflict is slipping beyond living memory – at the time of writing the last French serviceman of the First World War has passed away. Only three Britons who were in a war zone remain. Yet interest in a war that defined the course of the twentieth century and beyond has never been greater.

Academic and professional historians regard the First World War as an area of serious study – witness the establishment of the Centre for First World War Studies at Birmingham University, tours to the of the Western Front and coverage in the media, the number of books, papers and articles in the historical and popular press. There are many reasons for the growth in this interest: the expansion of genealogy, the study of the First World War and its literature in schools and increasing access to documentary evidence to name but three.

At the heart of the interest is the familial bond to the First World War. The half-forgotten conversations with elderly relatives, a faded photograph of a man in khaki or a torn letter from the front are powerful links that give many of us a reference point back to an event that changed the course of history. It is no coincidence that although there are many wide-ranging historical organisations in the UK, the Western Front Association has by far the largest participating membership.

There may also be something more profound at work. The twentieth century witnessed more significant change than any other time in the past in Western Europe, indeed arguably more than several previous centuries taken together. Studying the First World War gives us a view of a world now far removed from our own in terms of its values, technology, medicine, politics, and society – every facet of life in fact. Some look back with nostalgia, others appalled, yet all with the recognition that the First World War was played out by men and women whose human qualities are our own. When we know that Uncle Fred went 'over the top' in 1916, we wonder at his motivation, his old fashioned sense of 'duty', but we also ponder how we would have fared in his place – questioning whether we would have shared his courage, loyalty and powers of endurance and all those virtues and vices that are universally human throughout time.

During a visit to Fulwood Barracks, Preston, in 2001, I came across the records of Sergeant Samuel Mellor of the 8th Battalion of the East Lancashire Regiment, who was killed in the fighting east of Arras in 1917. Among the papers was a moving letter addressed to Mellor's widow from one of his fellow NCOs – Company Sergeant-Major James Fleming. Fleming and Mellor had both been wounded earlier in the war, meeting as part of a draft of men on their way to reinforce the 8th Battalion late in 1916. The papers had been deposited at Fulwood by Mellor's grandson Brian, who was passionate about his grandfather's war service and endlessly generous in his willingness to share his knowledge and materials with others.

A year later, Brian rang to tell me that the grandson of CSM Sergeant Fleming had that day visited him at home in Southport. Christopher Boardman had also uncovered Mellor's records at Fulwood and, in a moving gesture, Brian 'returned' the letter received by his grandmother over ninety years earlier to their writer's grandson. This kind act was typical of Brian, but also reflected his affinity and appreciation of the past and recognition that there are echoes that reverberate to this day. History, as it so often does, had come full circle. Sadly, Brian died recently, although not before Christopher and I had been able to present him with photographs of Sergeant Mellor's name recorded on the Arras Memorial. It is a pity that he will not see this publication, for without his interest and encouragement it would not have been possible.

Christopher Boardman had been researching the life of his grandfather CSM Fleming for some years before we met, at Brian's instigation. Intrigued as a child by the large picture of his grandfather and comrades hanging from the picture rail in the living room, Christopher remembered stories told in reverential tones of his grandfather's exploits during the First World War.

Although only two years old when James Fleming died, the tales Christopher later heard included talk of the award of the Military Cross, the Distinguished Conduct Medal and a visit to Buckingham Palace. Yet, through the stories he was told, a deeper fascination was born, a curiosity about, and empathy with his grandfather, whom it was supposed he physically resembled.

My own interest blossomed relatively late, in the mid-1990s. Knowing that my own grandfather had lost a brother in the First World War, I was perplexed to discover that 17378 Lance-Sergeant 'Jack' Barker had fought not with his native Cheshires, but the East Lancashire Regiment. A great aunt gave me his medals and memorial plaque before she died and I thought that was the end of it, until a trip to Fulwood Barracks at Preston uncovered only one item relating to the 8th East Lancs, a small diary sitting at the bottom of an otherwise empty box. That visit was the beginning. Another, to the great crassiers of the Loos coalfield on a pilgrimage to Jack's grave, cemented my commitment to find out more.

For over ten years we have gathered material from documentary, photographic, topographical and sound archives. Appeals for information appeared in all the newspapers in the Lancashire area, enabling contact with over sixty relatives of men who fought with the battalion. A website, overseen by Christopher's brother Philip, garnered interest from several individuals. A few could offer little, wanting to know more, others added greatly to what we knew. All were unceasingly kind and patient in the face of our seemingly endless questions! Inevitably, we talked mainly to relatives in Lancashire, but also from other parts of the UK, and to persons as far away as Australia, South Africa and the United States. We visited France and Belgium several times with Philip, walking the battlefields, interpreting the ground, trying to make sense of often complex events.

Living locally to Wigan, Christopher gained access to a large number of the obituaries of those who died. He and I selected roughly a fifth to include in this book, those that added something to the wider narrative and reflected the variety of soldiers' stories, occupations and backgrounds. A significant number of the obituaries are of men from the Burnley area, an indication of those contributed by Councillor Denis Otter. Christopher worked tirelessly, visiting numerous museums, libraries and archives. He was a regular visitor to Fulwood Barracks and the William Turner Archive at Accrington Library.

Living in Buckinghamshire meant that I was able to draw on material from the National Archives, Imperial War and National Army Museums. Much of this evidence is unpublished and appears in print for the first time. When examining documents at the National Archives, it was clear that the British Army was falteringly, and often with mixed results, attempting to learn lessons from the battles of 1916 and 1917. We have therefore included matter that adds to the evidence relating to the debate, christened 'The Learning Curve' of the British Army by Professor Peter Simkins and others.

Overall we have combined the essentially local with national and official documentary records. Primary sources have been used where possible and, when these were not available, eyewitness accounts from those who were present at the same time as the 8th East Lancs. We have aimed not only to explain what the soldiers did, but also why they did them, striking a balance between descriptions of events and examining their causes. It is worth noting that details of many of the events and analyses described in the text would have been unknown to the unit's veterans!

Christopher and I have written this book to draw together the remaining scraps of the history of the 8th Battalion; where it went, what it did and how its soldiers fought and died. It has not been an easy task. It was a unit belonging to no particular geographical location or social background, fighting with a division of no common origin, one of the few to leave no formal history. It counted among its own no significant writers, diarists or poets, nor did it figure significantly in that most infamous of actions – 1 July 1916, the first day of the Battle of the Somme. As a 'Service Battalion' it was low in seniority in the British Army and was disbanded before the war ended. Nevertheless, 8th East Lancs fought in some of the most difficult actions imaginable, at Arras, Passchendaele and of course in Picardy. In doing so perhaps 3-4,000 men passed through its ranks, almost 600 losing their lives.

Who were the men that made up the 8th East Lancs? From where did they come? The battalion history tells us a little more about its composition, relating that, of the early recruits 'a good many came from London, South Wales and Bournemouth itself'. This should not be taken out of proportion, for of almost 600 men who are recorded as having died with the battalion throughout the war, only five were born in Wales, three were Londoners and only one man was born in Bournemouth, with no others from the remainder of Dorset! Taken as a whole, the evidence tells us that the unit was composed largely of Lancastrians throughout the war. Over three-quarters of the men who died were born in Lancashire. Fifteen per cent came from other Northern counties, Scotland, Wales and Ireland. The remainder came from the rest of the UK, with one born in the US. Interestingly, over 40 per cent with the rank of sergeant were born outside Lancashire.

The average age at death of the men below the rank of officer was close to twenty-six years, with the most common age of death being nineteen, double the number of deaths of the next highest age. The oldest serving men were forty-eight, though those killed in their early forties were not uncommon. Unsurprisingly, the obituaries tell us that a considerable number worked in the cotton and its related industries. Many were employed as miners, engineers, railwaymen and in the production of iron and steel. Others worked in retail, running their own small shops, for co-operative stores or as salesmen. There were few white-collar workers: a small number of clerks, a stockbroker and a teacher. By and large, it was a battalion typical of many, composed of men from across industrial Lancashire, the North and the Celtic countries.

It is beyond the scope of this book to extrapolate trends from the obituaries. Nonetheless, some familiarity with the social context from which the soldiers came is useful.
Lancashire society before the First World War had been shaped by the cotton industry. Blackburn, for example, grew greatly in the nineteenth century, caused largely by an influx of Irish Catholic and non-conformist families looking for work in the mills. From the 1850s onwards, the Church of England's domination was challenged by the newcomers, whose churches had a significant impact on people's working and leisure hours, politics and education.[1] Churches of all persuasions saw it as their duty to improve the social habits of the working class. Competition between them meant that Sunday Schools, missions and churches sprang up across Blackburn, significantly influencing the lives of many. This was reflected in Lancashire as a whole and is

evident in the 1914–18 obituaries, where church-inspired activities appear to dominate people's leisure time. Sports teams, Bible classes, reading groups, choirs, music and theatre companies, pantomimes and concerts were often instigated and maintained by the churches.

By 1914, issues related to labour and class had taken over from religious concerns for many people. Nevertheless, the three remained closely connected. Trades unions in particular began to play a larger part in people's lives as urban development and industrialisation loosened the churches' influence. Many jobs were lost in the cotton industry at the onset of war and it was the unions that were able to cushion the blow for many families through the payment of full or partial benefits. A significant minority of 8th Battalion soldiers appear to have been active in cotton industry trade unions. Some of these men were also very energetic members of their local church, most notably Methodists and other non-conformists. Their interest in social justice through the fusion of the religious and the political was not uncommon at the time.

Ultimately, we have tried to describe to the reader what the soldiers saw, what the ground was like over which they lived and fought and to gain a little of what it was like to be there. There is some concentration on the battles – 'going over the top', the quintessential experience of 1914–18. Yet we have also tried to include a wide variety of source material to better reflect the battalion's whole experience on active service. The account is punctuated by brief pen portraits of soldiers, based on their obituaries. Each appears in the narrative as he died, echoing the Commonwealth War Graves Commission dictum that no account be taken of a man's military or civil rank, race or creed.

By its very nature an obituary is a partial portrayal of the life of the deceased. When studying them we were aware of their limitations as sources. This is especially true when the sheer number of deaths reported resulted in a formulaic approach to obituary writing. Not unnaturally, officers' letters to the families of those killed quoted in newspapers used phrases repeatedly. Expressions such as 'He was one of the most popular men in the company' or 'He was the cheeriest of lads' proliferate. Others were intended to soften news of the death of a loved one – 'most unfortunately a bullet struck your son below the heart killing him instantly'. The evidence often pointed to a man's final moments as anything but peaceful.

Obituary writers also accentuated what they considered to be the deceased's positive qualities, activities and deeds. Mention is made, sometimes implicitly, that a man was a good son or husband, popular at work and a stalwart for the local team. A link to a church is universally noted with approval. A common idiom employed is: 'He was connected with St Joseph's church.' Yet there are few clues to the extent of a man's faith and attendance at services. Therefore, we have chosen to include obituaries where the evidence for religious devotion, association with a trades union or zeal for football seems incontrovertible.

Their limitations accepted, obituaries are valuable in providing some insights into Northern Edwardian society. Loyalty to family, church and state are usually inferred. Details about employment, leisure pursuits, union involvement, familial relationships and church-going feature regularly. Enlistment particulars are given, as well as details of previous war service.

Some obituaries are included in this book because they contain an exclusive personal feature or a snapshot of life at home, or in the battalion. Often the details are pitiful: the wife bereaved six months after marriage, the parents seeking news of a missing son, or an orphaned child. Yet, the obituaries also portray a society at war: neighbours requesting financial support to look after the child of a widower, a recently married wife receiving news of her husband's death while on holiday and an impoverished spouse supported by charity living in a hotel. The authors believe that a study of the epitaphs of the First World War, in all their forms, is overdue.

This book signals the end of the beginning of our pursuit of the 8th East Lancashire. The research will go on and both Christopher and I would be pleased to hear from anyone with a similar interest, or who would like to know more. We can be contacted through our websites – www.8theastlancs.co.uk and www.galloping8th.co.uk.

Stephen Barker

1

BIRTH OF A BATTALION
1914–15

Early Formation

On his appointment as Secretary of State for War, Field Marshal Kitchener called for volunteers to expand the size of Britain's small, professional Army. Unlike many of his contemporaries, Kitchener believed that the war would be a long one and that it would require a much bigger force to face the larger armies of the Central Powers. On 6 August 1914, Parliament supported the raising of 500,000 additional men for the military. Three weeks later, the first 100,000 recruits of 'Kitchener's Army' had come forward and were formed into six divisions, referred to as K1. On 11 September, sufficient volunteers had come forward to form another six divisions – K2. So it continued, throughout the autumn of 1914 and into early 1915, six armies eventually being formed.

Kitchener had decided at an early stage that the county regiments would form extra battalions, in addition to their regular and territorial units, to accommodate the volunteers. These 'Service Battalions' were formed for the duration of the war, though they never enjoyed the same kudos enjoyed by the regulars.

The 8th (Service) Battalion of the East Lancashire Regiment was formed at Preston around a cadre of experienced soldiers in September 1914. The battalion was soon attached to the 25th Division, part of Kitchener's Third Army, which was forming around Codford, close to Salisbury Plain in Wiltshire. During September, the previously retired Colonel J.S. Melville was appointed to lead the battalion. He was joined by officers of varying experience and a number of veteran NCOs. It was only during October that the number of recruits began to rise significantly, though many of these men had initially enlisted into the Loyal North Lancashire and Manchester Regiments. This was related to the fact that these regiments shared Fulwood Barracks at Preston with the East Lancashire as an administrative centre.

One such volunteer was twenty-six-year-old James Fleming, a collier from Hindsford, near Wigan. Fleming enlisted into the Manchester Regiment on 5 October 1914 and was reassigned to the 8th East Lancs fifteen days later. This may have resulted from a surplus of men enlisting into the Loyals and Manchesters, while the 8th East Lancs were just beginning to fill their ranks. At depots like Fulwood Barracks at Preston, where overcrowding had been a serious problem in August and early September, men had been put on extended leave after enlistment to ease the problem.[1] Administratively, it made sense to reallocate men to battalions in need of recruits and get them into training, though one can only guess at the feelings of those whose choice of regiment had been ignored as they made their way to Codford during October 1914.

Above: Recruits taking the oath upon enlistment.

Left: Bt. Colonel J.S. Melville, who commanded the battalion throughout its training and early days in France.

Taking the King's Shilling

Those joining up were motivated by a number of reasons. Some did so for patriotic ideals and indignation at Germany's actions. Others felt that the war would be a short affair and enlisted to be part of a great historical experience. Events early in the war spurred men to join up – the retreat from Mons in August, the Battle of the Marne in September and the First Ypres in November all persuaded men that there was a job to be done and duty to perform in support of their countrymen across the channel. Others were motivated by the sight of the wounded returning from France. In many cases, the chance of escaping from hard and dismal employment was a key factor.

> This was undoubtedly one of the main reasons why the major industrial and mining areas produced such large numbers of volunteers, sometimes out of all proportion to their actual population.[2]

Life in the Army offered the chance of a permanent job with a steady wage. In Lancashire, the coming of the war exacerbated a decline in the cotton market, causing a short-term steep rise in unemployment as mills closed down or their employees were put on short-time working. In September, employers recorded that 90 per cent of men laid off had volunteered or had been called up as reservists.[3]

Some joined up to escape the clutches of the law, while others did so as a result of pressure from their employers or social superiors. Recruitment also offered the possibility of travel to new and distant places, away from their humdrum existences – a holiday in effect! Many young men enlisted because all their friends were doing so and they didn't want to be left behind and miss the adventure:

> When recruits of the 11th Lancashire Fusiliers left the Depot at Bury for Codford in Wiltshire, a great number of friends who had come to see them off thought that they too would like a holiday in the south and went too.[4]

Codford Camp, Wiltshire

Once in the Army the recruit was issued with a railway warrant and told to report to the regimental depot at Preston. There he might spend anything up to a fortnight receiving rudimentary training. However, Fulwood Barracks suffered from great overcrowding early in the war and it is likely that many men were quickly ushered on to the 8th Battalion base close to Codford St Peter and Codford St Mary. This was a new training camp to be used initially by the 25th Division. As the new soldiers arrived during September and October, they presented a motley sight, as one eyewitness in a neighbouring battalion remembered:

> About sixty percent had red coats and the rest civilian suits. A few had service dress, but no overcoats other than civilian ones. Hats were very various and included every form of civilian headgear. There were no rifles and no equipment. The effect, on parade of a man in a red coat, drab trousers and a bowler hat defies description.[5]

Although a comprehensive six-month training programme had been laid out by the War Office in August 1914, the inexperience of the officers and recruits, combined with shortages of equipment, meant that it was impractical. Training at Codford consisted mainly of 'Swedish Drill', a rigorous course of physical training, route marches and square-bashing on improvised

Rudimentary washing facilities, yet luxury by comparison with those available near the front line.

New soldiers collecting their palliases.

parade grounds. Fairly rudimentary attempts were made to introduce military formations, when practising for the attack, for example.

Initially, the men had to make do being accommodated in bell tents and there was a lack of basic equipment and sometimes food. For the most part these difficulties were overcome with the goodwill of the recruits eager to work together for the common good, and helped by the many kindnesses shown by the public at large. Yet goodwill had its limits and, as the good weather of September was replaced by continuous heavy rain from mid-October onwards, its reserves dwindled. Roads to the camps became impassable and training was suspended. Even route marches were impossible, the troops being soaked through before the last man of the company had struggled through the mud onto the road. The men had no change of clothing and no washing accommodation. There was nothing to be done day after day, but to lie in an indescribable state of mud, in tents without floorboards, listening to the rain beat down on the canvas. Rumours of other units training from billets in their home town began to circulate.

The month of November 1914 was marked by a wave of unrest among the battalions of the first three New Armies, Codford and Seaford being the worst affected. Mass meetings were held in the 25th Division at Codford and whole companies refused to go on parade. Trouble in the 11th Cheshire Regiment was narrowly averted by an issue of extra beer.[6]

Whether the 8th East Lancs were involved is unclear, but problems in the camps began to spread owing to the inclement weather, spurring the War Office into action. Since the beginning of the war, some regular and territorial battalions had been billeted in private houses and this policy was extended to include the New Army units.

Off to Bournemouth

As a result, the whole of the 25th Division decamped from Wiltshire early in November for placement in billets with the people of Bournemouth. The *Bournemouth Echo* of 9 November 1914, described the arrival of the division and the 8th East Lancs into the town:

> The first batch of the 16,000 troops, which are to be billeted in the Bournemouth District, arrived at Boscombe Station this morning. The troops who hailed from the Salisbury Plain district wore the familiar blue uniform of Kitchener's Army. The men appeared very fit and

New recruits being put through their paces.

cheerful, but bore unmistakable evidence of what camp life is like at this time of year. The North Lancashire troops are being followed this evening by the East Lancashires, the trains being due to arrive at Boscombe Station at 4.34 and 5.30 and at Christchurch at 4.14. The later arrivals getting out at Boscombe had their billets in the district around Pokesdown Station.[7]

It was in Pokesdown that the battalion was to stay until the end of March 1915. The nucleus of the battalion, made up of the cadre of experienced NCOs and soldiers, formed at Preston and those original Manchester and Loyals recruits represented perhaps only half the battalion strength. In the coming months, more volunteers would come to Bournemouth, swelling its ranks to the full complement of almost 1,000. The great majority of the men were to come from all parts of Lancashire, though there were small contingents of soldiers from other parts of the country. As the battalion history points out, the soldiers did not feel like the finished article:

> Very little equipment or uniform was available, the men being dressed in New Army Blues, or the old soldiers even in red, while as for rifles, a few antiquated Lee-Enfields were distributed to each company.[8]

In Pokesdown, the majority of the men were billeted in private dwellings, though some may have been housed in empty municipal buildings to save money. Empty houses were also pressed into service as a consequence. Initially, soldiers had to overcome prejudices held by some in the local population about the nature of their unknown northern visitors. Payment helped to assuage many of these feelings, with an allowance of 3s 4½d per day being the fee paid to householders per man. With soldiers and civilians living in such close proximity there were some difficulties experienced by both parties, though, as the *Bournemouth Daily Echo* was keen to point out to its readers, it was their duty to play a part at a time of national emergency:

> There have been discomforts and in some cases downright suffering in the process of formation, but the men have endured for their country's sake, just as their comrades are in the shell-torn trenches. The men have for a time emerged from these discomforts of camp

A group of 8th East Lancs soldiers during their stay in Bournemouth. Pictured standing on the left is Private Alfred Skipworth, who was killed in action in November 1916. Image courtesy of the Skipworth family.

training in bad weather and they are delighted to be in Bournemouth. It is for us to show that the country is proud of them.

    The personal welcome has been cordial – you see it in little incidents on the trams and in the street – and such a word means much to the men. Then in the billets there is a determination to make the men feel at home.[9]

A week later, another Bournemouth paper, the *Graphic*, felt confident enough to say how well the transition had been made from seaside to garrison town:

The appearance of the men as they entered Bournemouth was eloquent of the porcine conditions they had endured during too many weeks. Boots, clothes and shouldered blankets were woefully bespattered, with a mud which was not native to spic and span Bournemouth … and the unexpected character of the wearing apparel, loose fitting blue serge, with headgear of an appropriately rough type, enhanced the wonder of the spectacle. Candidly, these visitors, so travel stained and camp stained, excited a pleasure that was not unmixed with apprehension.

    But what a change was quickly wrought! Everywhere the men found billets to their liking in the houses of the residents, where hospitable attentions effected in their guests all that was required to make the necessary adaptation to their new environment. There is a general admiration of the men as a whole.[10]

To ensure that the 'admiration' continued, the civic authorities began to establish attractions for the soldiers during their leisure hours. Schools and halls were opened, providing reading and recreation rooms, and coffee stalls were set up. An appeal was made to the townsfolk for magazines and writing materials, as well as cards, games and books. Amateur entertainments were encouraged and the municipal orchestra organised special concerts at the Winter Gardens. Churches and charities were at the forefront of the effort and men of the 8th Battalion would have used the newly built YMCA hut close to Pokesdown Station.[11]

During the weeks prior to the first Christmas of the war, Bournemouth had a most successful season of entertainment. Unsurprisingly, performances of the pantomime 'Mother Hubbard' at the Theatre Royal played to full houses, as did the Hippodrome and the cinemas.[12]

Across the country, there were of course some problems when large numbers of 'foreign' young men were suddenly thrust upon a civilian population. Relationships could be strained when householders had been coerced into the role of landlord. Soldiers also had to overcome the prejudice of a civilian population as unfamiliar with immediate contact with the Army as most of us are today. Drunkenness was probably the most frequent cause of tension. To deny access to a concentration of public houses and other temptations, the authorities had insisted that there be no billeting in the town centre. It was also decreed that soldiers were not to be billeted on families without a male member of the household.[13]

From an Army perspective, another disadvantage of billeting was the time it took for a battalion to assemble each day. Conversely, as the men of the 8th East Lancs were scattered throughout Pokesdown, extra emphasis was placed on company and platoon work, with the result that officers got to know, and took added interest in the well-being of their men.

The winter of 1914–15 saw the battalion's training regime become more intense, reaching greater professional standards. The majority of the time was spent on drill, route marches and

Although taking a light-hearted view of their stay in Bournemouth, in reality men were only billeted with families where a male member of the household was present. Image courtesy of Ian Darlington.

The EAST LANCS. are "holding their own" at BOURNEMOUTH.

A first taste of bayonet training.

lectures. To these were added some night work, outpost duties, entrenching, bayonet fighting and musketry. The latter was still limited because of the shortages of rifles. The battalion history gives a flavour of some of the instruction:

> It is hard to recall what happened in those far off winter days of 1914 ... unless it be our bi-weekly attack on Foxbury Hill. That can never be forgotten. The long march there, then the assault and the weary return to billets; the outpost schemes on Warren Hill and Sopley common, or the nights we spent on Hengistbury Head repelling an oft invading enemy; or those days, those difficult days of company drill on Littledown Common, when cursing and being cursed, one thought one would never be able to understand its intricacies; or the guards that had been supplied on the foreshore, not only to watch for enemy submarines, but to be on look out for suspicious signals from the front and to prohibit the unsuspecting householders from showing naked lights.[14]

Fort Laira, Plymouth

The early months of 1915 brought many new men to the battalion. These volunteers came from the 3rd Reserve Battalion based at Fort Laira, Plymouth. Following enlistment, recruits were often sent to this unit to carry out their basic training. Groups of soldiers were then drafted out to the regular, service and territorial battalions, as the need arose. This continued throughout the war.

The 3rd Battalion became a home in England for the battalions at the front, and almost every officer and man of the line battalions served with it during some portion of those eventful years.[15]

Basic training at Plymouth lasted about two months for most recruits. A man enlisting in mid-November 1914, like Private John Barker from Northwich in Cheshire, could spend approximately eight weeks at Plymouth and then be drafted out to Bournemouth with the 8th Battalion at the end of January 1915. He could hone his skills for a further six months until the unit went to France. Soldiers recruited later on in the war trained for two months at Plymouth and went abroad straight away. Private William Timberlake from Colne was married on 27 January 1917, enlisted in February and was posted to France in April, after two months' training at Plymouth. He died of illness in August that year. Younger soldiers might train for a longer period at Plymouth. On reaching France, training continued, as veteran Thomas Heap remembered:

I joined up at Fulwood Barracks in the East Lancashire Regiment and was posted to Plymouth to a training battalion for six months. We were then moved by train along the coast to Folkestone for embarkation to France. I was nineteen years old at the time.

We arrived at Boulogne on 12 February 1917 and were marched to the transit camp on the outskirts of the town. We were then taken by train to Etaples, one of the base camps for the British Expeditionary Force. We had to undergo a further three weeks training in trench warfare. On completion I was then moved into the front line to join the 8th Battalion at Bethune.

The camp at Etaples was notorious for the sometimes brutal way in which men were prepared for the trenches. This was particularly resented by veterans who had been wounded, retrained and sent back to France. Their indignation was heightened by the fact that from 1916 onwards soldiers were redrafted on an ad hoc basis and sent to East Lancashire battalions other than the one in which they had trained and fought. Therefore, men reposted from the other East Lancashire units throughout the war contributed to its number. For example, Private William Young won the VC with the 8th after being wounded with 1st Battalion early in the war.

Training Intensifies

The spring of 1915 saw the training progress sufficiently that the 8th East Lancs took part in brigade exercises at Ringwood, in the New Forest. Here the battalion assembled for the first time since arriving at Pokesdown. It was at this time that soldiers began to work in earnest as a unit, getting to know each other and their officers better, as they prepared for war overseas. The significant officers were Colonel Melville, his second in command Major Magrath and the Adjutant Captain Hammond. There were other officers who would figure largely in the life of the battalion. One was 2nd Lieutenant Bentley, who would rise to lead a company. He would remain with the 8th Battalion throughout the war, the only officer to do so. Another was Lieutenant Archibald Yuille. Yuille was one of the many British officers who took a camera with him to war. Despite such pocket cameras being banned at the start of 1915, snaps seemed

The second-in-command, Major Beauchamp Magrath, who was to be killed in action in early June 1916. His loss was keenly felt by the battalion.

to have been taken with happy abandon throughout the Army. It was not only in the 8th East Lancs that senior officers actually turned a blind eye to the practice, with some of them posing for the camera! Yuille's images provide a unique insight into the battalion in the line during the period prior to the start of the Battle of the Somme.

Back in Bournemouth, the business of keeping young men gainfully occupied was a significant part of Colonel Melville's role. Sporting competition was important to this end and, in early March 1915, the battalion, along with the other units of 25th Division, took part in a cross-country running contest. Such activities were supported by the local authorities and added to the wider life of the town, as was reported in the *Bournemouth Graphic*:

Considerable interest was taken on Saturday in an inter-regimental cross-country team race at Bournemouth, in which no less than thirteen teams competed, each team consisting of thirteen runners. The race was held under the auspices of the Bournemouth East Sports Committee, who were kindly assisted by Colonel M. A. Kerr (OC King's Liverpool Regiment), Police Inspector Reasey and others.

A start was made at 3.59pm, and began at the *Queen's Park Hotel* for a distance covering a little over seven miles, the race finishing opposite the grandstand on the Boscombe Football Club ground.

An exciting run resulted in the King's Liverpool Regiment being the winning team, the placings being as follows:

	Pts
King's Liverpool Regiment	67
8th Loyal North Lancs	72
King's Own Loyal Lancs	129
8th East Lancs	141
King's Liverpool	166
Royal Engineers	337
King's Liverpool Regiment	351
Royal Welch Fusiliers	357
8th South Lancs	409
Army Service Corps	409

The prizes were afterwards presented by Col. M. A. Kerr, CB at the 7th Hants Drill Hall. Each member of the winning team was presented with a medal. Lieutenant Mallory received the cup, value ten guineas, on behalf of the King's Liverpool Regiment.[16]

One wonders whether any of the 8th Battalion wags, on returning to billets, commented on the winning of the cup by one of the organiser's own teams and from whom they received the award!

Windmill Hill, Ludgershall – April 1915

When the 8th East Lancashire had been attached to 25th Division in September 1914, it had been allocated as Army Troops. Such nominated units were chosen for garrison duties on the lines of communication, and for the security of GHQ and other major bases. Nevertheless, they received the same training as their fellow New Army Battalions. The East Lancs were not alone in being so designated. In Kitchener's first three armies, there were twenty-three such units attached as Army Troops. Many of these extra battalions eventually became Divisional Pioneer Battalions. Twelve of the rest, including the 8th East Lancs, were named as 44th Division at the

Grim-looking members of 6th Platoon, 'B' Company, photographed on 2 April 1915, prior to their move from Bournemouth. Second row from the front, three from the left is Private Thomas Jackson, and fourth from the left is his brother Private Joseph Jackson. Thomas Jackson has left a moving account of his time with the battalion prior to his death. Image courtesy of the Liddle Collection, Leeds University.

Warrant Officers, Staff Sergeants and Sergeants photographed at Windmill Hill Camp, Ludgershall in June 1915. Sitting at the centre of the front row is Colonel Melville. Standing second row from the back, three from the right is Sergeant James Fleming. In the same row on the extreme right is Sergeant Gawthorpe. Three rows from the back, two from the left, is Sergeant Skelly.

A group of 8th East Lancs soldiers at Windmill Hill Camp. Private Harold Darlington is seated fifth from the left. He died of wounds on 1 September 1915. Seated with his arms folded is Private Peter McNamara. One of the tents has been provided by Simonds Brewery from nearby Andover. Image courtesy of Ian Darlington.

end of March 1915. Two months later, 44th was renamed 37th Division, the parent unit of the 8th Battalion throughout the First World War.

So it was that in the late spring of 1915, the battalion was suddenly ordered to undertake training on Salisbury Plain in preparation for going to France. The 37th Division's units were to replace the 16th Irish Division, which had fallen well behind in its instruction schedule, as part of Kitchener's Second Army. As we have seen, the 8th East Lancs had been preparing since the previous September and were considered sufficiently ahead in their training to fill the gap.

While the 25th Division had been made up of mainly northern soldiers, inevitably the 37th Division had no geographical basis to its recruitment. It was made up of three brigades, each of four battalions – 110 Brigade was composed of four Leicester units, 111 Brigade of Fusiliers and Rifles, many recruited in London, and 112 Brigade. The latter consisted of 8th East Lancs; 11th Royal Warwicks; 6th Bedfordshire and 10th Loyal North Lancs. The four battalions would fight together until the spring of 1918.

The rumours of an imminent departure from Bournemouth proved to be true this time. Early in April, the East Lancashire platoons had their final photographs taken in Pokesdown. For many soldiers the stay in billets was, in retrospect, a happy part of their military service, sometimes with a doting family and the last time they were to have regular meals and a soft bed in which to sleep.[17] Their destination was the picturesque Windmill Hill Camp, close to Ludgershall in Wiltshire, a few miles from Andover. Here, on the eastern fringe of Salisbury Plain, the men returned to a life in bell tents and a more intensive training regime. The outdoor life in the summer of 1915 was a complete contrast to the battalion's time at Codford. The weather was good, the tents and facilities much improved and the men gradually came to greater health and fitness. There were still complaints about the quality and quantity of the food however, with mutiny breaking out in the neighbouring 152 Company, Royal Engineers.[18]

HEALTH AND STRENGTH.
August 21, 1915.
(Registered as a Newspaper.)

MARVELLOUS FEATS BY A MOTOR MAN.

HEALTH AND STRENGTH

EVERY WEDNESDAY 1d

JOB SHAMBLEY: HERO OF 100 FIGHTS

The cover of *Health and Strength*, 21 August 1915. Wrestling champion Private Jack Carroll referees another exponent of the art of Catch-as-catch-can wrestling, Private Job Shambley. His younger opponent is Private Peter McNamara. On the right of the picture is Private Harold Darlington. Image courtesy of Ian Darlington.

Commanding the 37th Division was Major-General Count Gleichen. He left an account of his early impressions of the new command:

> Lord Kitchener told me that I should have an excellent lot of battalions collected from the extra infantry units formed outside the already existing divisions … They were a charming variety, and lack of kit in those early days. At least two battalions were in blue; only one battalion had rifles complete, many had none at all and none was quite completely equipped. One battalion, indeed, arrived with nothing but water bottles and a few haversacks between them.[19]

However, from photographs taken in Bournemouth, it seems that the 8th Battalion was by this time wearing khaki for the most part. Gleichen also described the training undertaken by his battalions:

> We did as much as we could in the way of digging and trench warfare, but lack of material in sufficient quantities was rather against us, and there was nothing yet in the way of bombs, or gas masks, or trench mortars to play with: for these were only gradually making their way into training at home.
> But the main training was of necessity over ground, more especially as we thought it more likely that there would be plenty of opportunity for open fighting when we got to France, and hadn't pictured to ourselves nearly three years of trench and mud fighting. So we had plenty of brigade and open training of all sorts.[20]

However, as modern historian Peter Simkins points out, when referring to a description of one of 37th Division's manoeuvres:

A battalion of the 37th Division marching past King George V at Sidbury Hill near Tidworth, on 23 June 1915. Image courtesy of the Imperial War Museum, London. Ref. 78/69/1.

such exercises would have been more relevant to tactical conditions in the Franco Prussian War than on the western front.[21]

Rifle fire was also not up to standard, as Gleichen explained:

> Musketry, perhaps, was not quite so satisfactory: but that may be accounted for partly for the fact that we got our proper rifles so late and had little time to practise, and partly because the American ammunition with which we were served out (for practice only) was often found to contain little or no lead so that misses were by no means rare.[22]

There was time for relaxation too. In the 8th Battalion were a number of exponents of the art of catch-as-catch-can wrestling. This form of wrestling was particularly popular in Lancashire and many of the early wrestlers were miners by trade and worked in the East Lancashire coalfield of Wigan, Leigh, Atherton, St Helens, Golborne and Warrington. These men introduced wrestling to others in the battalion. In 1908, the first world tournament took place at the Alhambra Theatre in London. This competition pitted the best of wrestlers from the United States with their mainly British counterparts. Winning in the 10 stone category, and becoming world champion, was Jack Carroll, from Hindley, a Private in the 8th Battalion. Carroll was photographed looking on as another champion – Private Job Shambley – sparred with another recruit. In the short article for *Health and Strength* magazine Shambley's letter to a pal struck a confident note:

> Just a few lines to inform you that we are off to France forthwith. I enclose herewith an interesting photograph of myself wrestling with my Army pupil, Pte. Peter Macnamara, of Upholland, Wigan; Harold Darlington, immediately on the right, is my trainer. You will also recognise the referee, Pte. Jack Carroll, of Hindley, who won the championship of the world at the London Alhambra some years ago.

We are going to the front in the peak of condition. I scaled 13st 2 to-day. When we have whacked the Germans we will come home and do the goose step. We will not fail to have a real good time.[23]

Another 37th Division eyewitness, J.A. Johnstone, described the days at Ludgershall with fondness:

Those unforgettable days on Salisbury Plain, when my muscles ached until the one wish at the moment was for rest. The evenings, when off duty, one had the pleasant feeling that one could do as one liked, sit and smoke and talk, or go into the tent and rest at ease with thoughts for company. Those Saturday afternoons when we walked four or five miles to Andover to obtain the luxury of a real hot bath, have tea in a café there, spending money on little luxuries which we could ill afford on our pay of 1/- day, and then walk back in all the heat and dust of a country road in June, so that our arrival back in camp coincided with the sounding of the 'Last Post'.

Those lovely calm nights when we should have been in bed, sitting up and singing until 'Lights Out' sounded and one of the Camp Police would smack the canvas with his cane and call out in a rough voice to put the light out, on which the candle would be hastily blown out in dead silence instantly followed by loud snores to show we were asleep![24]

By the middle of June, the East Lancashires were fully equipped and took part in divisional manoeuvres around Hungerford. Unfortunately, they displeased the watching Major-General Gleichen by mishandling an 'assault' when handicapped by full pack and equipment. They were ordered to repeat the feat and to go back to basic training, which no doubt came as a blow to all concerned.[25]

Nonetheless, on 23 June, the entire 37th Division, including the 8th East Lancashire, was inspected by HM King George V at Sidbury Hill, a few miles from their camp. Two members of the division recalled the occasion. Roland Mountford of 10th Royal Fusiliers wrote home to tell his mother:

The whole division was inspected by the King this morning. He has been here since Wednesday, sleeping at nights in the train at Ludgershall Station. We rehearsed the whole business yesterday, the inspection taking place about three miles away towards the middle of the plain. Suppose there were about 20,000 men on parade. I was in the front rank and saw him very close to. He was on horseback and looked rather fit. Nevertheless, his face is very wrinkled and worried looking … I heard the King speak, you will not be surprised to hear he did it just like an ordinary man.[26]

Johnstone, in the neighbouring Rifle Brigade that day, gave a more exhaustive version of what he saw:

… being on a slight rise we could see the whole division, their bayonets flashing in the sun, while behind us, rank after rank, stood the wagons of the Divisional Transport and Artillery. As the King rode forward to the saluting base, a tall flag staff with the Royal Standard, the order 'Royal Salute, Present Arms' was given by the General Officer Commanding the division (Major-General Lord Gleichen) and the massed band played 'The King'. His majesty then rode slowly down the length of the parade and, returning to the base, took the salute as we marched past, Cavalry and Artillery first, the Infantry with their rifles at the slope and bayonets fixed. Wheeling into position, three cheers were raised for the King and, as they crashed out, our caps were raised on the points of bayonets and rifles above the cloud of golden dust rising from the trampling of 20,000 men horses and guns. His majesty bid us 'Farewell and God-speed' and as we returned to quarters he left by car for Ludgershall, escorted overhead by ten aeroplanes in battle formation.[27]

A representation in charcoal of members of 37th Division departing for France.

The small chateau of Nielles-les-Ardres. Some of the 8th East Lancashire officers were billeted here, and it was also the headquarters of 112 Brigade. The other ranks slept in nearby barns and houses during early August 1915.

France

The men from Lancashire now knew for certain that they were off to war. On 30 July, the East Lancs drew 250 rounds of ammunition per man. That day an advance party left Ludgershall station, with all the transport and vehicles. The following day, the rest of the battalion left on two trains for Folkestone. In total, the battalion numbered thirty-one officers and 854 other ranks. In Folkestone, Lieutenant Macqueen promptly arrested a man he suspected of spying, perhaps a sign of growing excitement. Yet it was not long before the battalion slid across a calm Channel under a full moon. They arrived at Boulogne just

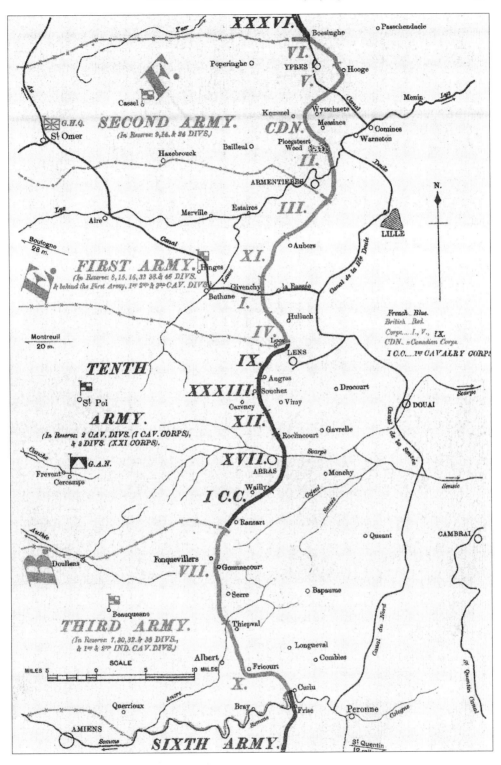

The Western Front at the end of 1915.

One of the bands of the East Lancashire Regiment.

after midnight on 1 August 1915, to be met by what one officer described as seeming like half the female population of the town. Next morning, the men paraded though the streets of the town behind the battalion band. There was just time to change money, buy a few souvenirs and send a postcard home before the men entrained, spending the next six hours in slow-moving trucks which took them in the direction of St Omer. They arrived at a small village called Nielles-les-Ardres, where they billeted in barns for the first time, the officers taking over the local small château. In this lovely spot, they had time to reflect on being abroad and the fact that they were heading to war. Here they experienced for the first time the sights of French village life that would become very familiar – the mairie, the spartan cemetery, the toiling peasant women and children struggling to run farms and the poplar-lined pavé roads. By 5 August, the battalion had reached the town of Hazebrouck, where for a time it would remain billeted in the shell of a half-built hospital. Here the men were to experience the first sights and sounds of war – enemy planes, anti-aircraft fire and ambulances bringing the wounded and dead from the front. However, the first fatality was not due to the Germans – 16662 Private Bradbury drowned in the canal on 15 August. Following inspection by General Plumer, the majority of the battalion marched fifteen miles to cross the Belgian border to Dranoutre, in order to provide working parties for trench-digging close to Kemmel and Locre, west of Ypres. The enemy inflicted its first casualties on the battalion at this time, light wounds caused by shrapnel, which no doubt caused excitement and comment.

The date 24 August saw the whole battalion head south by train into Picardy. It arrived at Doullens, after a long and difficult journey, and headed for the village of Mailly-Maillet, where the men were to prepare to take over a section of the line from French units. The battalion band, whose members were stretcher-bearers in the field, led the way …

> Their playing was fine and inspiring beyond all doubt, but their time, alas, was often at fault. Their instruments would run away with their legs, as it were, and the step would get quicker until the battalion, making heroic efforts to keep up with them, would finally give up the struggle and let them finish alone. No wonder we called ourselves 'The Galloping Eighth!'[28]

INTO THE TRENCHES
1915–16

Training for War

With the arrival of the New Army Divisions in France during the summer and autumn of 1915, the British were expected to take over greater responsibility for holding the Western Front. The 37th Division, under the command of VII Corps (Lieutenant-General Sir T.D. O'Snow), was in turn part of General Allenby's 3rd Army. The division was to take over positions from the French in front of the Picardy town of Pas, where its headquarters were to be situated.[1]

The French 58th Division, under General de Dartein, was to be relieved by the 37th Division during the period of 2–6 September 1915. 110 and 111 Brigades were to take over on the night of 3 September, with the British 48th Division on the right and the French 88th Division on the left. The East Lancashires and the rest of the men in the 112 Brigade had missed the opportunity to learn trench work alongside more seasoned regulars during August. However, their turn had now come. The battalion joined the 4th Division in front of the village of Mailly-Maillet on 31 August. Here the companies commenced their instruction in trench warfare for real. At 7.30p.m., nearly 800 officers and men proceeded into the trenches for the first time. They were taken by the experienced regulars up battered communication trenches into the support line. Old hands would later remember this baptism, when during the Battle of the Ancre in November of the year following, the battalion would follow the same fatal route to the Redan Ridge. The four Lancashire companies were distributed among the battalions of 12 Brigade. It was here that the battalion suffered its first casualties in action from shrapnel, grenades and aerial torpedoes. On the first night Private Vanden was killed and four other ranks were wounded, including the seriously injured Lance-Corporal Harold Darlington from the village of Greenfield near Saddleworth, who had enlisted in September 1914. Darlington was carried to the Regimental Aid Post by the stretcher-bearers, who doubled up as battalion band members. Desperate shouts for the stretcher-bearers were a regular feature of veterans' memories of their time at the front.

The Aid Post, run by a Royal Army Medical Corps doctor, was located in a dugout or trench just behind the front line. Here rudimentary first aid was given, a basic field dressing applied to Darlington's wounds and morphine administered to relieve some of his pain. A label was attached to the tunic, giving his personal details, information about his wound and any treatment administered so far. He was taken to the Advanced Dressing Station (ADS) several miles behind the front line. The journey on the stretcher, either on foot or more often a motorised or horse-drawn ambulance, was a difficult one – the casualty still being within the danger zone and the roads congested with men and vehicles.

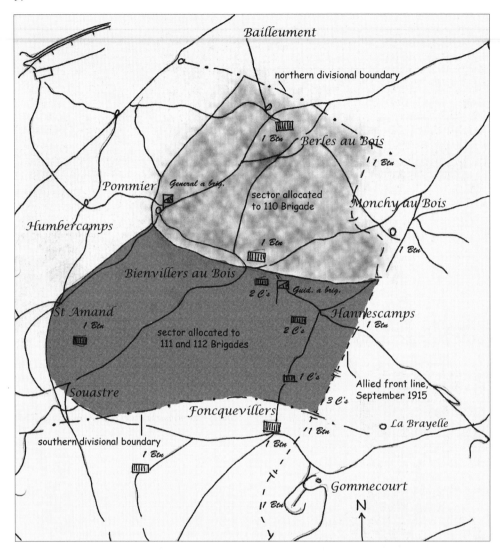

This map is based upon one distributed to 37th Division officers by their counterparts in the French 88th Division. It highlights the position of the French units to be relieved and the two brigade sectors to be occupied – 110 Brigade were to take the northern sector, while 111 and 112 Brigades occupied the southern. The villages in the rear areas were well known to all the soldiers of the division.

At the ADS, Darlington's dressing was changed and there was the possibility of further treatment depending on the nature of the wound. A serious wound usually meant that the casualty next took his turn for a place in the motor ambulance convoy to take him to the Casualty Clearing Station (CCS). The further a wounded man travelled through the casualty clearance system, the better his chance of survival.

In all, Lance-Corporal Darlington made a journey of approximately seventeen miles to the 4th Casualty Clearing Station at Beauval. Here was a large tented hospital consisting of up to 800 beds. The duties of the CCS were: to return the patient to the front line; transfer him to a base hospital in England for him to make a complete recovery and, if neither of these were possible, to give sufficient treatment to enable him to travel. It was at Beauval that Harold Darlington died of his wounds and is buried in the military cemetery which serviced the clearing stations there.[2]

Above: Stretcher cases awaiting their turn in field ambulances that would take them eventually to a casualty clearing station.

Left: Lance-Corporal Harold Darlington. Image courtesy of Ian Darlington.

The following day, 1 September, Sergeant Skelly from Liverpool was badly wounded. Skelly, like Darlington, made the journey to Beauval and was then transferred to one of the general hospitals at Etaples on the coast. These hospitals and the casualty clearing stations that fed them were close to the rail network to speed up the process of clearing the wounded.

At a hospital a man had a reasonable chance of survival and following treatment would be transferred to a hospital in the UK. Sergeant Skelly died at Etaples five days after receiving his wounds and is buried at the cemetery there – one of the 10,773 casualties of the First World War who died just short of returning to England.

Darlington and Skelly's deaths were a shock to their comrades. Word passed throughout the companies and later the whole battalion. Fanciful notions about the nature of war began to be undermined during this training period. Modern industrial warfare, as one veteran put it, was a 'grim, unsatisfactory, bloody silly business'.[3]

The 8th East Lancashires finished their period of front line training on 2 September and three days later headed for the Foncquevillers sector that would be home to the battalion in the coming months.

'Funky Villas'

The 37th Division took over the French trenches on a line from Foncquevillers in the south, to German-held Monchy au Bois in the north. Between the two lay the community of Hannescamps, also in allied hands. The area was just north of the Somme Department, but is usually associated with the eponymous battle of 1916.

The land was agricultural, open and gently rolling, enclosed by expansive fields of the type to be found in parts of East Anglia today. Nevertheless, it was foreign to the eyes of men from industrial Lancashire. The rises and falls of the ground concealed some movement from both sides, yet during daylight mobility was often difficult and dangerous. Orchards, copses and small

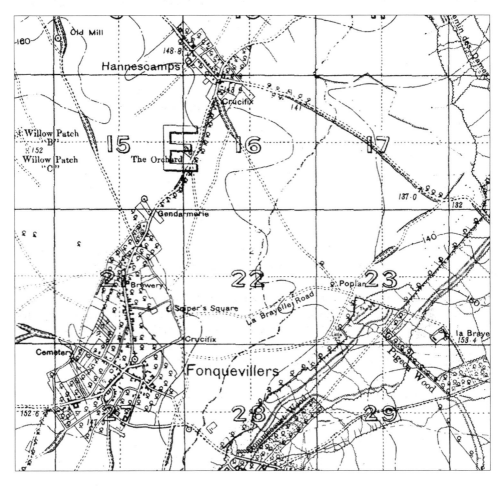

The front line at Foncquevillers and Hannescamps was occupied by the battalion from September 1915 to the beginning of July 1916. Image courtesy of Fulwood Barracks.

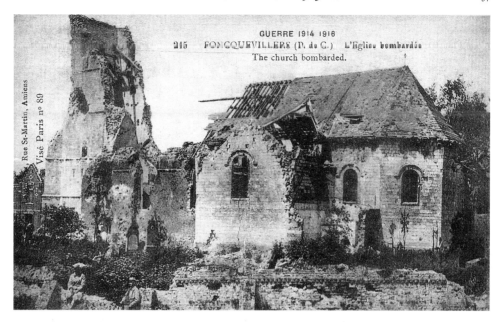

A French postcard depicting Foncquevillers church in 1916.

coverts bordered the extremities of each village, larger areas of woodland punctuating the horizon. Depending on their mood, Foncquevillers was known variously to the men of the 8th as 'Fonky', 'Funky Villas', 'Fonkin-bleedin' Villas' or in extremis 'Fucking Villas'! In September 1915 'Fonky' had been spared the worst excesses of war. Seven hundred yards behind the Allied line, the eastern side of the village was clearly visible to the Germans opposite, machine-gun fire raking the length of the Hannescamps road. Many of the houses in Foncquevillers were damaged, some little more than heaps of bricks. Many were farm buildings, constructed in the traditional manner around a central courtyard. The church was in ruins, its roof missing and the cemetery despoiled. Cellars were used by troops in support of the front line. Indeed, throughout this period the Mayor of Foncquevillers lived in one such cellar, keeping up a census of available holes, known as the 'list of billets'. The majority of the villagers − les Foulquois − had left earlier in 1915. On the western fringes of the settlement, the French had established an Advanced Dressing Station and a small cemetery. The 37th Division took over its running and it is in this cemetery that the Lancashire men were interred during their tour of duty.

On 16 September, the 8th East Lancashire was ordered to relieve the 10th Royal Fusiliers. Their scouts led 'A' and 'B' Companies past the church and into the communication trenches leading down to the front line. 'C' Company was in support in 'Snipers' Square', a series of dugouts from which a good view of the line was to be had. 'D' Company remained in support in the cellars under the ruins. The battalion history describes the position:

> By 11 pm the relief was complete and for the first time the battalion was holding its bit of the British line. After a quiet night, dawn came, enabling us to look around and inspect our trenches more thoroughly. 'A' Companies line consisted of two portions, the South Fortin and the North Fortin. The latter a kind of outpost trench connected to the main line by a short communication trench. 'B' Company held the next straight southerly portion of trench.[4]

The British front line hugged the single contour between the Germans and the village. 'A' Company front formed a salient, both sides of which were protected by the saps called the

The High Street in Foncquevillers as it was in the autumn of 1915. Image courtesy of the Imperial War Museum, London. Ref. 0677/1. Also Mr Tom Yuille.

'Fortins'. Here men looked due north, south and east. Then the line curved away to the south straightening to face the looming shape of Gommecourt Wood.

The French trenches were not what the battalion had come to expect during its training. The parapets were thin and their depth was insufficient for British requirements. However, they were in good condition with spacious dugouts, which held wire-netting beds, though the roofs too were thin and barely able to withstand the blast of a grenade. In this sector the French and Germans had observed an unofficial 'live and let live' policy, preferring not to upset their own peace by disturbing the neighbours opposite. Though the battalion would lose many casualties here, the sector was still considered to be relatively peaceful throughout the war.

About 200 yards across the low valley lay the German positions. As was customary, the Germans were able to fashion the best possible sites for defence, sacrificing ground here and there to claim the high ground or some other desirable feature. Opposite Foncquevillers, up the rising slope, lay no less than five lines of trenches. Directly opposing the Lancashire men were strong points, known to the allies as the 'Big Z' and 'Little Z', so named because of the shape of the line as it hugged the contour, a hedge line and possibly the fringe of a small copse. The Zs enclosed a strong point called the *Schwalben Nest*, or Swallows' Nest, by the Germans. Here they had built an intricate maze of trenches protected by barbed wire in which to site their Maxims. This was the dominant feature of the German line opposite Foncquevillers, one that the 8th would find hard to crack.

The 37th Division line was divided into two sectors. To the north, opposite Monchy au Bois, it was held by the experienced men of 110 Brigade. The southern Foncquevillers sector was allotted to both 111 and 112 Brigades. The sector was divided into three battalion portions, the middle unit with all four companies in the front line, the flanking battalions with two companies in the firing trenches and two in support. One battalion remained in brigade reserve. Thus it was on that first night that 'B' company not only held the furthest-right flank of the battalion, but also the brigade and the division! After six days in the front line 'A' and 'B' Companies exchanged positions with 'C' and 'D' until the whole of 112 Brigade went to rest. Such was the early experience of the 8th – twelve days in the trenches and twelve in reserve, billeted behind the line. This pattern would continue throughout 1915 and into the spring of 1916.

Casualties

The saps, known as the North and South Fortin, provided an advanced position from which to observe enemy movements. They were dangerous positions to hold and the two deaths of the East Lancashire's first tour of duty came in the exposed South Fortin position. On 21 September Sergeant Henry Davidson was shot through the neck and heart and Private Harry Knowles was mortally wounded in the stomach. Both were musicians. Davidson was a foundry worker from Blackburn. He had been a territorial soldier, a member of the National Reserve and was a former policeman. As a euphonium player in the police band before the war, Davidson helped the chaplain of 112 Brigade organise outdoor services, providing musical support that the Reverend H. Sturt obviously valued, as he made clear to Davidson's wife:

> Your husband was well known to me and helped me many times with the band. He was a fine and brave soldier. We buried him by moonlight yesterday at 9pm. The Colonel and Major of the regiment were present. Henry Davidson is buried at Foncquevillers Military Cemetery.[5]

Major Magrath too wrote to Mrs Davidson, telling something of the esteem in which her husband was held by his colleagues. Yet, as the casualty rate increased, so higher-ranking officers and padres of brigade found it impossible to replicate this generosity.

> Your husband was well known to me, both as one of our best bandsmen and also as one of our best sergeants. He was proved by his company commander to be an excellent and most trustworthy non-commissioned officer, which makes his loss felt all the more. I had

Sergeant Henry Davidson. Image courtesy of the *Blackburn Times*.

just left him for we had been seeing after another wounded man in his section and he was going back when he was hit in the heart and head. He was buried in the cemetery just behind the line. All the officers and sergeants who were off duty were present. We have put a cross on his grave marked 'Sgt Davidson, 8th East Lancashires' with RIP and the date above it.[6]

Davidson lies in Foncquevillers Military Cemetery. He was forty years old, one of the oldest men in the battalion. The wounded man mentioned by Magrath was Private Harry Knowles from Cloughfold, near Rossendale. He was a twenty-nine-year-old father of three. Originally a carpet printer by trade, he earned a living as a quarryman prior to the outbreak of war. He had played the violin in Warburton Brothers Orchestral Band and like Davidson was probably involved with the musicians of the battalion. Knowles was taken to the hospital at Henu, five miles from Foncquevillers. Another chaplain, the Reverend A. Gordon-Wrigle, describes Knowles's last moments to his wife:

September 22nd 1915. Private Knowles died in hospital yesterday after being fatally wounded in the stomach. I am the Church of England Chaplain attached to the Field Ambulance, and I was suddenly sent for by the commander of the hospital and I found your husband in a critical condition. He was unconscious, but while I waited by his bedside, he suddenly came to and I spoke with him and did all I could do for him. He was very easy in mind and after a little talk he understood who I was and told me that he was not afraid to die. It was extremely sad, yet very wonderful. I called to see him the next morning and the doctors told me that he was very bad, but might last a few hours. He was sleeping quite peacefully and half an hour after I left he passed away in his sleep. I buried him last evening after dusk in the civil cemetery of the village in which the hospital is situated. [7]

First Tour of Duty

The first fortnight in the trenches was typical of life in the front line during their time at Foncquevillers. Patrols were sent out to establish the nature of the ground in front and the enemy dispositions. Working parties were employed improving the parapets and mending the barbed wire entanglements. Even those companies in support were required to provide working parties of 100 men to work with the Royal Engineers. There, too, were moments of excitement:

8th East Lancashire Regiment opened a concentrated fire on a tree in which a sniper was suspected to be lodged. At the third volley he fell out of the tree onto the ground.[8]

To be worthy of entry at a divisional level tells something of the novelty of such an event at this time.

Approaching the time of the Battle of Loos on 25 September, men were ordered to cut zigzag passages through their own wire, in case an opportunity of a breakthrough occurred further north. Private Austin became the third mortal casualty in the battalion, again shot dead in the South Fortin, a place associated no doubt by the troops with ill omen! On 28 September, the 8th East Lancashire was relieved and marched back to a tented camp at Humbercamps. Two days later they requisitioned barns in St Amand. Their first tour of duty was over.

An 8th East Lancs party working on the Berles Redoubt, behind the line north of Hannescamps 1916. Image courtesy of the Imperial War Museum, London. Ref. 0677/1. Also Mr Tom Yuille.

Behind the Line

Behind the front line were settlements used during 'rest' periods out of the trenches. Approximately two miles away were Bienvillers and Berles, while further back beyond the Corps Line* were the communities of Souastre, St Amand and Humbercamps. Their farms, houses and barns became well known before the end of 1915.

Time spent in billets and rest camps generally constituted at least three-fifths of an infantryman's service with his unit on the Western Front.[9] Men were generally billeted on farms, sometimes abandoned, occasionally still occupied by family members. Built around a single courtyard and protected by four walls, the men lived in the barns, sheds and outhouses, sleeping on straw, often with the smell of animals about them. Made of wooden frames, supporting wattle and daub walls, these buildings offered some shelter and were a relief after the trenches. Yet many were damaged, filled with holes, and the men inside took shelter under their waterproof sheets. Repairs to the barns were ordered before the winter weather took hold, parties working under the supervision of local French plasterers.

Any idea that the East Lancashire men had that they were in for a restful time was soon dispelled. A rigorous programme of work and training was to be carried out.[10] In addition to digging defensive positions around the villages and in the Corps line, other tasks included musketry training; route marches and rigorous physical exercises. Drill in rifle and grenade use was also stressed and there were to be lectures and discussions on 37th Division trench orders; scouting and sniping techniques, the repair and draining of trenches and the importance of sanitation. Personal hygiene orders were also very precise: each battalion was to have the 'baths' at the town of Pas made available to it for one day. Bathing was compulsory for all ranks and the 8th Battalion were ordered there late in September, their first task since leaving the trenches. Parties of 80 men were ordered to arrive every 40 minutes. As two eyewitnesses remembered:

Each bath involved a long and tiring march. On arrival we went to an old dye works or brewery. In the building were a number of large metal vats, in each of which 10 men were expected to disport themselves. By that time we had been living near enough to nature not to find anything incongruous about this. The bath included an issue of alleged clean underwear. The clothes had been washed out, but being old were generally bad in colour and infected with eggs. The Army laundry authority was never able to destroy these eggs effectively without making the wool so rotten as to render the clothes unwearable.[11]

At Pas were the divisional baths; once a week we were sent in fatigue dress to the brewery, where the men pranced in enormous vats and the officers lowered themselves cautiously into narrow tanks filled with a boiling liquid of suspicious colouring.[12]

The Last Months of 1915

In October the battalion said goodbye to Colonel Melville. Formerly retired officers like Melville, who had been called upon to form New Army Battalions, were replaced by newly promoted men; regulars who had over a year's experience of trench warfare. Others found that their health gave way – their own experience conversely not preparing them for the front line. The battalion was saddened to lose a man who had formed it almost a year ago to the day. He was replaced by Lieutenant-Colonel Mackay, a regular officer from the 1st Hampshire Regiment.

A local boy under arrest and guarded by a member of the 8th East Lancs. Pommier 1916. Image courtesy of the Imperial War Museum, London. Ref. 06/77/1. Also Mr Tom Yuille.

As autumn turned to winter, so the familiar routine continued: a fortnight in the trenches and a fortnight out at 'rest'. Casualties were few, only eight men wounded in October. Yet the condition of the trenches in front of Foncquevillers became wretched. In places they became impassable where walls had collapsed, at others the water was waist deep. Men were forced out of the communication trenches onto the top and tried using the farm tracks and roads, leading to an ever-greater number of casualties. A new communication trench was dug by the battalion connecting the village to the front line. 'Red Rose Lane' was dug at night under enemy fire and incorporated trench boards, drains and sump pits. The rain continued to fall and so too did the German shells in November and December. Aerial torpedoes, *minenwerfer** and rifle grenades fell on the East Lancashire positions in increasing numbers. But it was the living conditions that tested the men. At this time the battalion history claims that they 'kept extraordinarily fit and cheerful'.[13] An entry in the war diary tells a different story:

December 7th 1915

Weather continues very bad and trenches are up to the waist in water. Reliefs in the fire trenches take place by companies every 3 days (instead of the usual six) owing to the weather, it being impossible for the men to stand the strain any longer.[14]

Private William Young VC

The awarding of the only Victoria Cross in 8th Battalion occurred at this time. During the night of 21 December the state of the fire trenches had been so poor, with men continuously moving about in water, that the decision was made to exchange these platoons with those in support every twenty-four hours to avoid the onset of trench foot, widespread illness and the further lowering of morale. Perhaps, owing to the fact that the trenches were impassable, Sergeant Allen of 'B' Company moved above ground and was struck in the thigh by a German sniper. Allen shouted to Young to stay where he was, but with no thought for his own safety the latter mounted the parapet, rushing forward under heavy fire and was immediately hit in the face by a bullet that shattered both jaws, removing the lower one. In spite of these terrible wounds, Young pulled him back to the 8th East Lancs lines with great effort and with the assistance of Private Green, who had also left the safety of the line under fire. Reputedly, Private Young then made his own way back to the dressing station where it was discovered that another bullet had pierced his chest. As the citation to the Victoria Cross stated:

The great fortitude, determination, courage and devotion to duty by this soldier could hardly be surpassed.

Private Green received the Distinguished Conduct Medal for his part in the rescue of Sergeant Allen, who in civilian life had been a professional golfer. Private Young, originally from Glasgow, had joined the Army just prior to the Boer War. He served until 1902 and joined the Army Reserve on his demobilisation. On enlistment in 1914, Young was living with his wife and eight children in Preston. He was part of 1st Battalion, being wounded at the First Battle of Ypres in November 1914. During the Second Ypres in April 1915, he was badly affected by poison gas and returned home to recover. The vagaries of the depot system returned him not to his beloved 1st Battalion, but to the unknown 8th in the winter of 1915. He was in the trenches for practically the first time at Foncquevillers when he saw Sergeant Allen fall.

After returning to England for treatment, he was accorded a civic reception in Preston and £500 was raised for the benefit of his family. He undertook three operations for his

Private William Young VC, hoisted on the shoulders of fellow wounded soldiers during his temporary recuperation, before succumbing to his wounds on 27 August 1916. He is buried in New Hall Cemetery at Preston. Image courtesy of the *Northern Daily Telegraph.*

wounds and wore a prosthetic mask during his many public appearances in Preston. However, William Young suffered heart failure during the third treatment and died on 27 August 1916 in a Cambridge hospital. His funeral was the best-attended Preston had ever seen and he was interred at New Hall Lane Cemetery, one of only two First World War VCs to be buried in the UK. Private Young never received the award; it was accepted posthumously on his behalf by his widow from the King at Buckingham Palace.[15]

Like many heroes he was extremely modest about his achievement and even his wife knew nothing about it until congratulations began to shower upon her after the *London Gazette* publication of 30 March 1916. She would later write:

> I could never draw from my husband an account of how he won his VC, only what you already know, but I want to tell you that he was a 1st Battalion man with 17 and a half years' service. I do not want him to be published as a 'Kitchener man' as he was a reservist at the outbreak of the war.[16]

This telling comment says much about the way in which the regulars viewed the 'New Army' men, even as late as 1916.

Christmas Patrols

Patrols will be sent out nightly from each company front. They will be given definite orders as to what information is required of them. Patrols must be aggressive and must immediately deal with any German patrols met. In addition to their role of obtaining information, it is their duty to keep NO MAN'S LAND clear of hostile patrols.[17]

This clear statement of intent was laid out in 37th Division's standing orders and, during the Christmas period of 1915, the 8th East Lancashire was ordered to fulfil it to the letter. The High Command had been eager to avoid a repetition of the Christmas truce the year earlier, when many divisions had been involved in fraternising with the enemy. Perhaps too, they believed that New Army Battalions might be susceptible to such interaction. Whatever the motive, patrolling by the battalion increased during the latter days of 1915 and was replicated by the Germans. A bombardment on Christmas Day was ordered, to which the latter replied in kind, causing not a few casualties in East Lancashire ranks. The day was brightened only by deliveries to their lines of hampers by 10th Royal Fusiliers. The 'Stockbrokers' battalion of this regiment was one of the first 'Pals' battalions and their ranks were made up mainly of men from the professional classes. Winston Churchill numbered among their officer ranks for a short period in early 1916.

Patrols could vary in purpose: either they were for listening to the enemy just beyond his wire, or patrols were armed to the teeth with an array of hand-to-hand combat weapons to attempt to dominate no man's land and if possible return with prisoners. This could be a hazardous business as the patrols on the night of 27–28 December found out:

An 8th East Lancs sentry using a trench periscope at Foncquevillers 1916. Image courtesy of the Imperial War Museum, London. Ref. 06771. Also Mr Tom Yuille.

Above: Probably posed, an 8th East Lancs sniper in action. Image courtesy of the Imperial War Museum, London. Ref. 06/77/1. Also Mr Tom Yuille.

Left: Private Wilfred Entwistle. Image courtesy of the Walter Holmes Collection.

Our front was patrolled throughout the night under Lieutenant Winser, 2nd Lieutenants Bentley, Hollick and Koekkhoek and Sergeant Shakeshaft. None of these patrols encountered any enemy patrols. Winser took a machine gun accompanied by Koekkhoek with a covering party. They patrolled the valley between the lines opposite Foncquevillers for three hours without meeting anyone. The ground near the German lines is very swampy and in parts under water. While this patrol was out an enemy machine gun opened fire, rifle grenades were fired back in reply, while our machine gun opened fire over the heads of our patrol at the Maxim nest opposite. The enemy replied by throwing bombs from his front trench in addition to rifle and machine gun fire.[18]

The patrol was complimented on its good work by their Brigadier.

The Trials of Private Thomas Jackson

As 1916 began, one man had other worries on his mind than shot and shell. While out at rest at Souastre on 28 January, Private Jackson of 'B' Company found time to write to his neighbours in Burnley. Ada Read and her husband George had been looking after Jackson's wife, who was seriously ill and taking care of his four-year-old son Wilfred at the Jackson family home in Sandygate Street, close to the mill where Thomas had worked as a weaver. In the billet from where he was writing was his brother Joe, who had joined up at the same time.

Friday night January 28 1916

Dear Jud and Ada,
Just a few lines hoping that they find you all in the best of health as I am in the pink just at present. I have been expecting a letter for a long time now but have not got one for this last four weeks. I am very glad to hear my little lad has got quite well again and going on alright. We are out of the trenches at present. We came out on Tuesday night after another bad do, we had three wounded and one killed in my platoon and we had about 24 casualties altogether. We have still the same old wet weather and I hear that you have had your shair (*sic*) in Burnley. The last time we was out of the trenches I sent you a post card with flags on and one for our Wilfred and one for your Clara and one for Mrs Sagar. This is 18 days ago since I sent them. I hope that you let me know if you have got them. I did laugh at that letter your Clara and our Wilfred wrote. I am writing this in bed up in the corner of an old barn. Our Joe is grumbling over the candle or else we will have none left for morning and it is spitting blood now so no more at present. Hopeing you write back soon from your most sincere friend Tom. Good night and God Bless you all. (*sic*)

Wilfred XXXXXXXXXXXXX ClaraXXXXXXXXXXXXXXXXXXX[19]

Jackson wrote home again on 2 March, this time from Humbercamps. Following the usual pleasantries he wrote:

I had a bit of a shake in the last place when they was bombarding (*sic*) a aerial torpedo burst not far from where I was and they are murderous things I can tell you, but I have got over it. We are billeted in a farm just behind the firing line. We are in supports (brigade reserve) and today we are stood to all day ready to move at a moment's notice. I have been expecting a letter from you this last few days. I hope that there is nothing wrong with my little lad again. I know there as been measles again in Burnley and all passes has been stopped to there for a

Captain Paul Hammond.

while. (*sic*) Dear old Pall I am about fed up with this life and wish it was all over. I am sleeping in the place where the farmer had his pigs and believe me it is the best place I have had for months … I hope that you will write back first thing old Pall as I am dying to hear over our Wilfred.

The New Year brought fresh tours of duty and increasing casualties. On 8 February the Germans fired over 200 shells of all calibres into the Lancashire trenches and 'Snipers' Square'. Signaller Private Wilfred Entwistle, a twenty-six-year-old man from Accrington, was killed. One of the many soldiers in the 8th who were regular attendees of non–conformist churches, Entwistle's spiritual and social life was built around the Baptist church he had attended as a boy, first at Sunday School, then in the choir and finally as an active member of the young men's institute. He was also a member of the church Liberal Club. As an unmarried man, Wilfred's life was divided between these pursuits and his job as a taper at the Accrington mill where he worked. He is buried at Foncquevillers Military Cemetery.[20]

The battalion's officers began to suffer too. While it is unlikely that Entwistle travelled beyond the borders of his native county, Captain Paul Hammond had travelled widely. On 19 February, both Hammond and Lieutenant Winser were killed by a sniper. Paul Hammond had been born in Brazil, but educated at school in England. His learning had continued at the School of Mines in Saxony, where he had developed his passion for geology. After returning to Brazil, he had spent his twenties making mineralogical surveys of various parts of that country, before returning to England to enlist at the outbreak of war. Adventurers of this type were typical of the age and an asset to the New Armies. Winser's audacity had only the day previously won him the green card* for meritorious service. Hammond is buried at Etretat churchyard, about twenty miles from Le Havre, while Winser is interred at Doullens Communal Cemetery Extension No.1.

Divisional Rest

Finally, at the beginning of April, the 37th Division earned a long-expected rest. The East Lancashires spent the next three weeks drilling and training for the assault on the Somme in July. Compared to the fortnightly cycle of front line, support and reserve there was a little more time to relax. Nevertheless, the Army liked to keep its men fully occupied, allotting them a daily schedule during their time out of the line – believing that the devil really did make work for idle hands. In spite of this, soldiers found ways of recuperating and taking their minds off the war.

In place of the village 'pub' was the estaminet,* which served watered-down beer and wine and egg and *pommes frites* to the Tommies. Sometimes a willing pianist would play the hits of the age late into the evening (last orders were usually at 8.30p.m.!). The 8th Battalion ran a canteen in Bienvillers. This ramshackle wooden affair sited near to the church was run by the officers. Here the men could buy hot drinks, newspapers, writing paper and pencils and sometimes treats such as marmalade and sauces to embellish the daily rations.

When any opportunity presented itself soccer was played. No British battalion travelled without footballs and the 8th Battalion were no different. Within half an hour of the completion of a long route march a football would be produced and kicked about in a desultory fashion. Football allowed an escape from the strain for trench warfare and allowed them to undertake an activity that was an important part of their life at home.

Men took the opportunity to write home, sometimes sending back any pay they had saved and reflected on life in general. Following a long illness, Thomas Jackson's wife Eliza died early in April. Jackson himself was allowed compassionate leave to attend the funeral and make arrangements for the long-term care of his son Wilfred. On returning from Burnley, he wrote with regret once more to George and Ada Read, from Sus St Leger on 29 April:

The officers of 8th East Lancashire photographed in France early in 1916.

I have not been well since I came back as I was inoculated in the right breast 2 days after I landed back and it really puts me out. (He then goes on to explain how the quartermaster is helping him with Army welfare payments for Wilfred) I should have made the arrangements before I came back but when I am in drink I think of nothing. There was lots of things I ought to have done while I was at home. (sic)[21]

The Barn Owls

One other form of entertainment well known to the East Lancashires was the divisional concert party called the 'Barn Owls', which had been established in a newly created theatre at St Amand during September 1915. The men from Lancashire would have related to the Pierrot costume traditionally associated with end-of-the-pier entertainment seen at Blackpool, Southport and Morecambe. Created under the patronage of the divisional commander, the troupe toured the area, led by pianist Lieutenant Haynes and the star turn George Young, a baritone singer with a powerful voice and extensive repertoire. As Lieutenant-Colonel Collinson of 11th Royal Warwickshires remembered:

The band and performers were selected from men of histrionic ability, and apparently there were many candidates, as those chosen were quite up to London music hall standards.[22]

The first shows were improvised and spontaneous, involving topical sketches, songs and dancing associated with the music hall entertainments of the time.[23] The 'girl' initially played by Private Cameron of 13th Rifle Brigade was, it was alleged, quite good looking and 'she' was admired by the 112 Brigade Transport officers in particular! When the curtain went up the troupe would launch into:

We are the Barn Owl Boys,
We make a lot of noise,
We come here nightly,
We just can't get to Blighty,
We are just Divisional toys.

Don't think that we're shirkers,
We fight like Leicesters or Gurkhas,
We've got our iron rations,
And all the latest fashions,
We dig like real good workers.

One theatre goer remembered the building:

The divisional concert party performs in a large barn in St Amand. Inside it was like a church; three aisles divided by wooden pillars and would seat 300 men. Civilians attended too. The cast in action did wonders as stretcher-bearers … they deserve medals galore for the manner in which they helped to keep up our morale and divert attention to the brighter side of life.[24]

The 'Howls', as they were sometimes known, had transformed the building with curtains, footlights, a ticket office and seating on an assortment of pews from churches recently evacuated by their congregations.[25] The temperature in the barn was often very cold, but the entertainment was a warm and welcome distraction from the war. At the end of the evening the 'Barn Owls' would finish with:

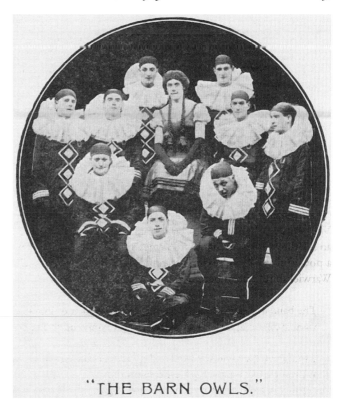

"THE BARN OWLS."

Members of 'The Barn Owls', 37th Division concert party. Their Pierrot costumes are typical, as is the 'leading lady'.

We hope you will excuse us,
If you didn't like our show don't abuse us,
For we tell you straight and true,
That like you we're soldiers too,
We don't get any suppers, any more than you.

And why we're not in the trenches just now,
Is because our Gallant Staff,
Have sent us here to try and make you laugh,
But one and all,
We are ready for the call,
To join our regiments.[26]

The 8th East Lancashire returned to the trenches on 2 May for one more trench tour at 'Funky Villas'. During their time at Sus St Leger they trained hard in preparation for the 'Big Push' further south in Picardy in the summer. The role of the grenade in trench warfare had grown in importance since 1914, overtaking the emphasis placed on musketry fire. The men attended the grenade school and undertook detailed training in the use of bombs and smoke grenades. The specialist grenadiers undertook a nine-day course. Lectures and instruction were given on such themes as types of grenades, their accurate throwing, care, storage and cleaning, rifle grenades and catapults, bombing up occupied trenches and grenade mechanisms.[27] By a sad coincidence, the first three deaths on their return were self-inflicted. Private Smith, Lance-Corporal Everett and Corporal Robertson were killed together when grenades accidentally exploded. All three were buried at Foncquevillers, the last to be buried there.

Hannescamps

In readiness for the assault on the Somme, the 46th Division took over the trenches at 'Fonky'. The 37th Division 'side-stepped' north as a result, leaving the East Lancashires holding the trenches in front of the village of Hannescamps, half a mile north of their previous position. Across no man's land the Germans held the rural community of Monchy au Bois. The distance between the trenches tapered from 200 yards at the southern end to no more than thirty across from the northern platoons. Here soldiers became used to some communication with their enemy as the divisional diary recorded:

> South of Monchy enemy were very talkative, remarked on our fur coats, enquired when we were going on furlough and ended by asking for cigarettes.[28]

Another eye witness recorded a similar interaction at Hannescamps:

> We heard some shooting on our left flank where the British line ran into a salient. The sound carried clearly on the cold air. 'Hallo Tommee,' cried a German voice, 'are you soon going home on leave?' 'Next week,' the Englishman shouted. 'Are you going to London?' was the next question 'Yes.' Then call at two-two-four Tottenham Court Road and give my love to Miss Sarah Jones.' 'I'll go alright and I'll jolly well …'. The fate of the lady was eclipsed in a roar of laughter from our side and the angry splutter of a machine gun from across the way.[29]

It was during this time that a small notice was set up in no man's land by the Germans and was brought in by one of the 8th Battalion. It was a piece of propaganda and referred on one side to the capture of Kut by the Turks and the resulting 13,000 British prisoners in Mesopotamia (Iraq). On the other, the veracity of Foreign Secretary Grey, Prime Minister Asquith and Earl Kitchener was questioned. Most topical of all, the sign referred to the alleged murders of unarmed German U-boat sailors by HMS *Baralong* and of a Zeppelin crew by those of a British trawler the *King Stephen*. Both incidents had occurred in the last six months and were referred to in both countries' papers.[30]

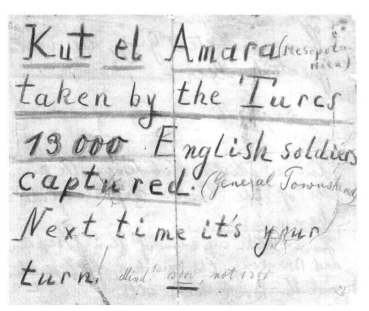

One side of a small propaganda notice left in no man's land by the Germans and recovered by Lieutenant Archibald Yuille of the 8th East Lancs in May 1916. The sheet refers to the capture of General Townsend's force, which surrendered to Turkish forces at Kut in the Mesopotamia Campaign during the previous April. Image courtesy of the Imperial War Museum, London. Ref. 10752 Misc 101 (1559).

Death of Magrath

The Hannescamps sector was constantly bombarded throughout May and June by artillery, trench mortars and rifle grenades. The Germans knew of the forthcoming battle. Their aeroplanes had spotted both the fresh artillery batteries and newly dug jumping-off trenches in no man's land. The accuracy of their weapons was now more potent because of the close proximity of the trenches around the notorious 'Fallen Tree Corner'.

On 2 June, having been on leave for some time, the battalion second-in-command Major Magrath was making his way down Collingwood Avenue with Captain Hallet of the divisional artillery. They were going to assess ways in which the front line might be protected from the trench mortar batteries opposite when a shell fell on top of them, killing them instantly, along with Hallet's orderly. Magrath's orderly was badly wounded. Private Pat Conway from Farnworth wrote home to tell his wife what had happened:

> I had just written a letter and was giving it in when they passed me with the best man in the division on a stretcher, who had been talking to me about an hour before telling me to see him when we got out of the trenches. He was our second in command and a captain and an orderly were also killed with the same shell. Soon after two of us were told off to dig a hole for him.

As he dug Magrath's grave, Conway went on to relate how near he himself came to death and the effects on men of modern artillery:

> We had not been at it ten minutes when a shell came. We just heard it in the air and dropped with our faces on the ground, but it was too late. It dropped eight feet away and we both expected

The pipe-smoking Major Magrath, photographed at Mondicourt in 1916. Image courtesy of the Imperial War Museum, London. Ref. 06/77/1. Also Mr Tom Yuille.

Corporal Arthur Brown. Image courtesy of the Colne Roll of Honour.

being in ribbons, but something made me creep away on my stomach, as other shells were falling. I was dazed when I came to myself at the foot of the crucifix I told you about. Of course all this happened in a few seconds, but it seemed hours to me. Some men came expecting to find us in bits, but the shell was a dud. It drove the man silly who was with me and they had to take him down the line to hospital.[31]

Conway's high opinion of Magrath was shared by all in the battalion, to whom it was a great blow. Lieutenant-Colonel Collinson of the neighbouring 10th Loyal North Lancs recalled Magrath as cheery and convivial and noted his death with regret. The son of a Major-General, forty-four-year-old Magrath had been a regular soldier in the Indian Army. During 1914–15 he had served in the Cameroons, but returned to volunteer for service in France. He was a professional soldier and knew how to get the best from his men, who adored him.

Magrath's orderly was Corporal Arthur Brown from Colne, a nineteen-year-old weaver who had been involved in the Scout movement before the war, acting as bugle bandmaster to the Holy Trinity Scouts. Perhaps because of his youth, Brown had been allocated as orderly to a surgeon at one of the Divisional Field Ambulances, before taking up his role acting for Magrath. An orderly was, in British Army parlance, an officer's uniformed servant, supposedly taken on as a voluntary extra duty, for which service the officer paid. In addition to his normal duties, he was responsible for the officer's clothing and kit and also for preparing and serving meals. In the trenches, an orderly carried his personal weapon and often acted as a bodyguard while the officer carried out his duties.

Major Beauchamp Henry Butler Magrath was buried at Bienvillers Military Cemetery, not far from where he fell. Brown died of his wounds the following day in the hospital at Doullens.

Preparing for the Big Push

The role of the 37th Division on the immediate left of the forthcoming attack in Picardy was laid out in Divisional Order No.23 and dated 22 June:

> The 46th and 56th Divisions will attack Gommecourt. A preliminary bombardment will be carried out for a period of five days and the infantry attack will be on the sixth day, commencing at time zero. These days are to be designated by the letters U to Z.
> The 37th Division will cooperate as follows:
>
> Gas. Eight of the 20 cylinders per emplacement along the whole line are to be reserved for Z day. The remaining 12 cylinders per emplacement are to be discharged at the first favourable opportunity from V day onwards. The object of these discharges is to catch the enemy unawares. They will be accompanied by smoke, or by artillery, machine gun or rifle fire. Success depends on silence and secrecy.
> Smoke. Smoke discharges will take place on W, X, Y and Z days. On Z day the smoke cloud will commence five minutes before zero hour.
> Active defence in order to make the enemy expect an attack of the 37th Division front. For this purpose both the 111 and 112 Brigades will during the five days preceding Z day bring Stokes Mortar, machine and Lewis guns to bear on the Monchy salient, with the object of inducing the enemy to believe that he is going to be attacked there.

From 16 June onwards, the battalion was involved in moving the gas cylinders down to the trenches at Hannescamps. This was hard and dangerous work, two men carrying the heavy

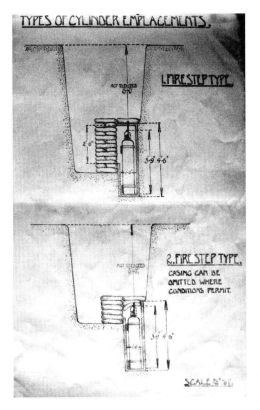

Diagrams illustrating two possible placements of gas cylinders in a trench.

In Monchy.

German soldiers posing for photographs in their gas masks at Monchy au Bois.

cylinders slowly down the communication trenches to the firing line at the rate of 100 yards an hour. Men later remembered their aching shoulders and arms that resulted from carrying these dead-weights on poles. In addition, instructions were issued to lie over the cylinders in the event of bombardment to prevent premature detonation and the ensuing loss of surprise that would have resulted! Special emplacements were dug for the cylinders at the front, though the instructions made clear that in an emergency they were to be leaned up on the fire step and discharged from there. During bombardments soldiers wore their gas masks in case a cylinder ruptured.

One man who was becoming particularly desperate was Private Jackson. Having recently attended his wife's funeral in April, and feeling that he had failed to make all the necessary arrangements for his young son, he wrote a letter to George and Ada Read, who were looking after the boy, from the trenches at Hannescamps. It was to be his last.

Tuesday June 20th 1916
Dear Jud and Ada,

Just a few lines hopeing they find you all in the best of health as I am still in the pink. I have been expecting a letter from you for a long time. You might write and keep me informed how my little Lad is going on. I think everybody has forgotten me now, as I hardly get any letters now, so just write old Pall and let me know how he is going on. I get all sorts of things in my head when I don't hear over him. You must let me know also how you are going on over money and if you are getting it every week. I keep going to the Quartermaster and asking him over it, but he says nothing has come from Preston yet. We are back in the trenches again, we have only been out for six days and we was in for 18 days before that. I am getting about fed up with this and wish it was all over. You must look out for a big battle with the British shortly and I shall be in it. Well I shall put my trust in the Lord to come through as I have done before. If I go under it will only be like the thousands as done before. Wile I write this the Germans are bombarding us, but they little know what is in store for them, we have some tackle here that will blow them back to Berlin ...

Good afternoon and God Bless you all.
don't forget to write. (*sic*)

On 26 June, close to midnight, Jackson and the majority of those men in the fire trenches withdrew to the support line, while those left behind donned gas hoods or box respirators. Machine guns and ammunition were wrapped in waterproof sheets and the entrances to dugouts were covered with Vermoral Sprayer Solution. Royal Engineers entered the trenches and released the gas. The grey cloud of chlorine blew slowly across no man's land. A German eyewitness, Lieutenant Ernst Junger of Fusilier Regiment 73 described the scene:

Round about midnight, all hell was let loose in the curved front enclosing Monchy. Dozens of alarms clocks rang, hundreds of rifles went off and white and green flares went off unceasingly. Next a barrage of fire went off, heavy trench mortars crashed; drawing plumes of fiery sparks after them. Wherever in the maze of ruins there was a human soul, the long drawn out cry went up: 'Gas attack! Gas attack! Gas! Gas! Gas!' By the light of the flares, a dazzling flow of gas billowed over the black jags of masonry.[32]

The gas brought an instant artillery bombardment in reply on the East Lancashire trenches. Rifle grenades and machine gun fire also came, though miraculously only one man was mortally injured among the many hit. One of the wounded men, Sergeant James Fleming of 'D' Company, held one of the hottest spots on this part of the front adjacent to 'Fallen Tree Corner', the closest point on the salient opposite to Monchy. As the Lancastrians sheltered from the barrage, Fleming was quick to spot a shower of rifle grenades land in his traverse and shouted to his men to take cover. In doing so he was hit in the side and foot by an iron splinter. His officer wrote to Fleming's wife telling her that:

It is largely through NCOs of your husband's type that the new armies have been such a success.[33]

Colleagues in the sergeants' mess agreed with these sentiments when one of them penned the following verses in honour of 'Jim' the following day, 27 June:

A band of sergeants five were we,
Two Jims, two Jacks and one teddy,
The comradeship was rare and fine,
Both back at rest or up the line,
The seeds of friendship early sown,
Is now a rare thing fully grown,
Through various time of strife and stress,
We still retained our sergeants' mess,
Till one dark day the deed was done,
The break was made, we lost just one,
Twas dear old Jim from Tyldesley Bongs,
A jolly good singer of some rare good songs,

Private Jack Boller. Image courtesy of the Jewish Military Museum, London.

Private Smith Chadwick. Image courtesy of the Bacup Museum.

Twas quite a joke with our old S.M.
To hear him say 'The old favourite Jem',
It happened in the front line trench,
This sad and painful, mournfull wrench,
Old Jims foot got in the way,
A piece of shrapnel gone astray,
Found therein a resting place,
And now we miss his dear old face,
And of his company now bereft,
There still are four comrades left,
And for the sake of good old times,
The next time we go up the lines,
We will avenge our comrades fate,
We'll stop the old Huns hymn of Hate.

Although evacuated to England for treatment, it was not to be the last time that twenty-eight-year-old Fleming, from Atherton near Wigan, would risk his life for his men.

The morning after the gas attack, as Sergeant Fleming passed down the line for treatment, across in Monchy Ernst Junger wandered about the ruins:

The next day, we were able to marvel at the traces the gas had left. A large proportion of the plants had withered, snails and moles lay dead, and the horses that were stabled in Monchy for use by the messengers, had watering eyes and muzzles … rattled civilians had assembled outside Colonel von Oppen's quarters and demanded gas masks. Instead they were loaded onto lorries and driven to towns and villages set back from the front.[34]

8th East Lancs soldier in the trenches at Hannescamps 1916. Image courtesy of the Imperial War Museum, London. Ref. 0677/1. Also Mr Tom Yuille.

The ongoing bombardment of the enemy continued unabated. The German positions were plastered with high explosives and shrapnel. It was the greatest barrage in history. At the last minute, it was decided to dig a shallow jumping-off trench halfway across no man's land on the front of the three divisions in the Gommecourt sector. This would halve the distance to be covered by the men on Z day. The 37th Division did so to keep up the pretence that they too would be in the attack.

On 29 June, gas was once more released from the 8th East Lancs' trenches. The resulting counter-barrage resulted in the deaths of six men. Among them was Private Jack Boller from Whitechapel in London. Boller was one of the few Jewish soldiers to die with the battalion during the First World War. Also killed instantly by the same shell was forty-two-year-old Private Smith Chadwick from Stacksteads, near Bacup. Better known as 'Jerry', Chadwick was a stoker on the locomotives at the stone quarry where he worked. His family circumstances were particularly pathetic. His wife left to care for his seven children, aged between three and seventeen, and Chadwick's own elderly, crippled mother. 'Jerry' Chadwick's life was hard and perhaps a factor in his enlistment – the opportunity of a brief escape from the drudgeries of his existence. Both Boller and Chadwick are buried in Hannescamps New Military Cemetery.

Just before dawn on 1 July, the East Lancashire bombers crawled out into no man's land and occupied the recently dug shallow trench, halfway between the front lines. They lay for some hours until a perfect, cloudless and warm day dawned. At 7.25 a.m. the men threw forward their red phosphorus-filled grenades and lit the smoke candles, which they supported between sandbags on the parapet. A wall of acrid smoke rose high into the air. On 37th Division right, opposite Foncquevillers, the men of the 46th East Midland Division advanced through the smoke towards the 'Z' and Gommecourt Wood. They hardly reached the uncut German wire and suffered severe losses. Their General was sent home in disgrace. Allegations were made that some of his men had not left their trenches and that the 37th Division diversionary tactics were bungled. The next day, the battalion was relieved. The men knew that their turn was coming.

3

OVER THE TOP:
THE SOMME – 1916

Au Revoir to 37th Division

At the same time that 37th Division was releasing smoke on 1 July, further south, astride the old Roman road linking Amiens and Bapaume, the 34th Division launched their attack. The objective was the German front-line position of La Boisselle. They were then to push on towards the highest point on the ridge, the German second line and the village of Pozières. The 34th sustained 6,380 casualties that day, the highest of any division; 102 (Tyneside Scottish) and 103 (Tyneside Irish) Brigades were shattered. They were exchanged with 111 and 112 Brigades for rest and recuperation and to regroup and retrain with new men in a quieter part of the line. The East Lancashires were going into the heart of the battle.

They rested in billets until the morning of 5 July, when twenty London charabancs hove into view. The men hadn't been told where they were going, but many guessed that they were 'in for it'. A few would only require a one-way ticket. The buses:

> were noisy and here and there, where the drab khaki of the wartime paint was chipped, a glint of red still hinted of the days when they had plied along Oxford Street … The windows were boarded up, but, miraculously, on some the conductors bell was working.[1]

Initially, the men sang heartily, glad of the change of scene. They encouraged their drivers to overtake the buses in front, to hurtle them down the pavé roads along some stretches. Finally, and in spite of the discomfort caused by the buses' inadequate suspension, the men dozed until their arrival at Millencourt, after a seven-hour journey. Here the battalion's officers were briefed that evening by 34th Division staff. It would be September before 111 and 112 Brigades would rejoin the *Golden Horseshoe* Division, a fact much regretted by their senior officer and many of his subordinates.[2]

> The rupture was a blow to us all. The division was very efficient, and in its own opinion, was far more suitable for a breakthrough than a break up.[3]

However, this view was not wholly shared by all of Major-General Gleichen's staff. Gleichen never led his division during an assault and was replaced at the beginning of November 1916.

The process of removing incompetent commanders was continuous and, in October 1916, Sir Henry Wilson (IV Corps) was asked by Horne, his Army commander, if Major-General Count (later Lord) Gleichen 'was fit to command a division on the Somme', and consulted other

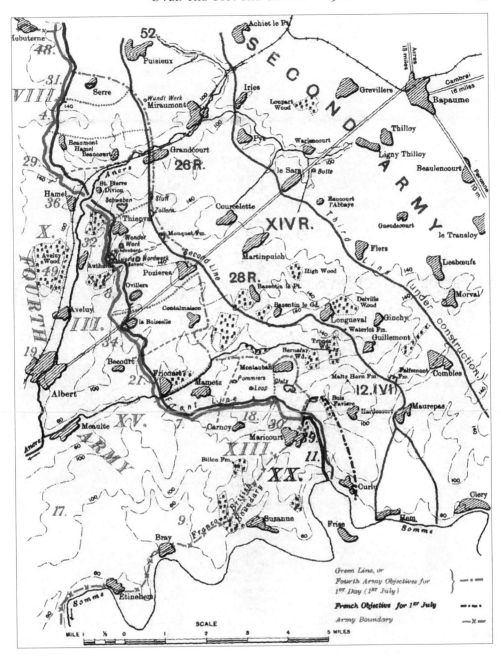

The Somme front on 1 July 1916. Pozières was an objective that day, yet the 8th East Lancs lost over 350 casualties assaulting it on 15 July. Both 111 and 112 Brigades were brought in to relieve those of the 34th Division.

officers for their opinions. General Sir Charles Ferguson (XVII Corps) was somewhat evasive, but Major-General Sir Reginald Barnes (116 Brigade) and Colonel Berkley Vincent (GSO1, 37 Div.) indicated that they had no confidence in Gleichen, because he was 'stupid, pig-headed, & blind'. As a result Horne wrote to GHQ requesting the replacement of Gleichen, who was sent home 'having been found unfit to command a division in the battle' by Haig, who reported that the staff of the division were 'all pleased to have got rid of the Count'.[4]

It seemed that although the men of 111 and 112 Brigades were needed at the Somme battle their senior officer was not. Usually, whole divisions relieved each other. The break up of the 37th Division was the first indication that Gleichen's skills were not valued, leading to his ultimate removal.

Up the Line

On their arrival at Millencourt, the men of the 8th East Lancashire Battalion had more immediate concerns. The camp was full of other 111 and 112 Brigade units and there were neither rations to be had, nor tents to accommodate them. After a miserable night in the rain, the men were issued with full rations of ammunition and copious amounts of grenades. The emphasis placed upon bombing during their training in April was about to be tested. The 111 and 112 Brigade units marched to Albert and passed below the hanging Virgin and Child on their way up the Bapaume Road. On the Tara-Usna Ridge, a panoramic view of the German lines was to be had. To the east lay the Lochnagar Crater, the great mine exploded near La Boisselle opposite 34th Division. All around, black dots could be seen, the bodies of 34th Division men killed on 1 July. Ovillers to the left and Fricourt to the right were in ruins. The battalion left the rest of the brigade and spent almost two days in the open at the rear of Bécourt Wood, where the men watched a stream of wounded brought up to the casualty clearing station in a nearby chateau. They also witnessed a steady flow of the dead from the chateau to the wooded cemetery, where a number of padres worked continuously.

At dusk on 7 July the battalion moved up Sausage Valley and took its position in the reserve trenches close to the crater, where carrying parties were needed for the front line. The bombardment here was intense for three days and included lachrymatory shells*. The use of respirators added to the woes of the men already laden with ammunition and supplies.

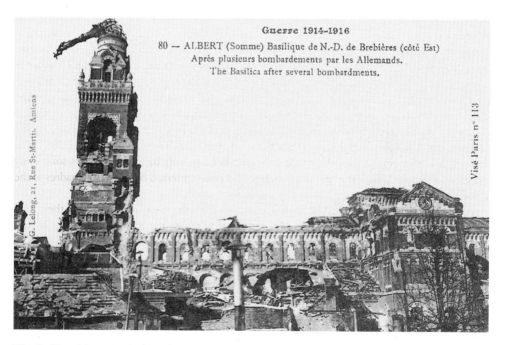

The Basilique Notre Dame de Brebiéres. The 8th East Lancs passed under the hanging Virgin and Child on their way to the front line in early July 1916.

Private John Hall. Image courtesy
of the Denis Otter Collection.

Private John Hall, a twenty-eight-year-old weaver, was killed by shellfire on 9 July. Hall, originally from Burnley, had left his family and country to make a new life for himself in America some nine years earlier. Like many men of his generation, Private Hall sought to exploit the potential opportunities offered abroad, not only in the US, but also Canada, Australia and Britain's other Dominions. In 1914, some men joined the armies of their adopted countries, yet America's neutral stance until April 1917 forced many former British subjects across the border into the Canadian forces, or, as in Hall's case, back home to Britain. At the outbreak of war, and still lacking funds to pay for the trip, he worked his passage across the Atlantic to enlist. He spent a day with his father at his former home in Burnley, joined up the following morning and left for his depot the next afternoon. The feelings of his father, who had lost his other son at Loos the previous September, can only be guessed at. His son's body made its last journey back the way the battalion had come, interred by one of the padres in the wood at Bécourt.[5]

As the German line was pushed back, sometimes from the west, at others from the south, those trenches previously occupied by the enemy were put to use by the British. On 11 July the 8th moved up into that part of the German defences called the Brown Line. This trench system ran at right angles toward the enemy still holding out in Ovillers to the west. Enfilade fire caused many casualties as the men tried to cut fire steps and deepen the position for protection. Two days later, the battalion relieved the 10th Loyals in the front line trenches running parallel and adjacent to the La Boisselle-Contalmaison road up to Bailiff Wood. One company was in a more advanced position around the fringes of Contalmaison Wood. Ahead lay the village of Pozières, about 1,200 yards away. The village was the key to the German defences on the Somme, occupying the highest point in the German second line and sitting astride the road to Bapaume. The lads of the 8th East Lancs were indeed 'in for it'.

A Confused Picture

At 3.20a.m. on 14 July, the Battle of Bazentin Ridge opened with a five minute hurricane bombardment of the German second line between Delville Wood and Bazentin-le-Grand village. The success of the attack came as a result of the surprise achieved, the timing of the assault and the brief yet intense bombardment. These features would ultimately be identified as important factors in gaining success on the Western Front.

In the East Lancashire positions about Contalmaison Wood, the ground shook and the horizon to the west was emblazoned with flashes of white light. Twenty minutes before this barrage, at 3a.m. and in complete darkness, Lieutenant Macqueen took out a patrol towards Pozières in support of the forthcoming attack. This platoon consolidated a position in a trench on the southern perimeter of the village. Another patrol of platoon strength came up in support led by 2nd Lieutenants Speak and Dunmell. The reports these patrols sent back added to an increasingly confused picture as to whether the village was held by the Germans or not. The ground covered in the dark was unknown to the officers and men in comparison with the Foncquevillers front. The 34th Division War Diary makes it clear:

> An officer's patrol from 112 Brigade entered the enemy trench just south of Pozières and found it to be unoccupied and in good condition.[6]

This is almost certainly referring to an 8th Battalion officer. However, Lieutenant-Colonel Collinson, commanding 11th Royal Warwicks, was unsure just where the patrols had reached:

British infantry prepare to go over the top.

Lieutenant-Colonel Mackay (8th East Lancashire) told me that his patrols had succeeded in reaching the south-west outskirts of the village. Probably they mistook the trenches some distance this side of the Lisière (village boundary) for the actual village line, as subsequent events showed that it required something like a division to get into the place, and the vigilance of the enemy would hardly have tolerated the presence of a patrol there.[7]

In addition, during the afternoon there was a dramatic turn of events. Reports from an artillery observer reached 34th Division HQ, via its parent III Corps that the Germans seemed to be evacuating Pozières in great disorder.[8] Whether the Germans were evacuating wounded, or a relief was taking place is unclear. But as a result, and to take advantage of the vacuum, the ongoing bombardment was halted and more patrols were ordered to push into the village itself. At 7p.m., 2nd Lieutenant Stout and his party approached along the main road, arriving at a barrier erected across the highway into the village from Albert. A party of Germans was spotted. Two were bayoneted, but a third escaped to raise the alarm. All hell let loose. Along the southern fringes of Pozières, from the orchards and houses, machine-gun fire forced back the patrols to their starting points with a number of casualties. It was a taste of what was to come the next day.

Taking part in the patrol was Lieutenant Archibald Yuille. Born in Calcutta, where his father had been in the tea business, Yuille was brought up in the UK, being educated at Rugby school. He had been with the battalion from the outset, taking a camera to record what he saw and, in so doing, providing the only photographic testimony of the 8th East Lancashire at war. Yuille was to be wounded at Pozières, thereafter joining the Royal Flying Corps. He would later gain fame as the first pilot to shoot down a Gotha bomber at night in the summer of 1918.

Lieutenant Yuille would later recall the events of 15 July 1916, an important eyewitness to what happened that day.

Planning for Attack

At noon on 14 July, Operation Order No.84 was received by 34th Division from III Corps, directing an attack on the German second line, north and west of Bazentin-le-Petit. This assault was to build upon the successes of the Bazentin Ridge battle that morning, maintaining momentum and keeping up the pressure on the enemy. The 34th Division was to co-operate in this action by gaining ground towards Pozières.[9] The attempts by the 8th Battalion patrols throughout 14 July, described above, were aimed at holding trenches close to the village in order to provide a jumping-off point close to Pozières for the attack on 15 July. The fact that the patrols had been dislodged and retired meant that the distance to be covered amounted to about 1,200 yards.

In the early hours of 15 July, Lieutenant-Colonel Mackay received the specific orders from GOC* 34th Division Major-General Ingouville-Williams that 112 Brigade would attack at 9.20a.m. after an hour's bombardment of the village. Later, at a brigade conference, Mackay and his fellow battalion COs made the detailed arrangements. They are worth looking at in detail in order to understand what happened that day:

112th Infantry Brigade Operation Order No.36 issued at 3.50am 15/7/16

Pozières village is reported to be lightly held by the enemy. The 1st Division, which is on our right, is attacking at 9am today the German second line as far northwards as a point 500 yards east of Pozières. The 25th Division (on the left) will bomb up the communication trenches leading to the western edge of Pozières commencing at 9.20am.

The 112th Brigade will attack Pozières from the South-Attack to commence at 9.20am.

The Objective of 112 Brigade in the first instance will be the German trench between the CONTALMAISON-POZIÈRES and the BAILIFF WOOD-POZIÈRES roads. The leading battalion will then advance in to the village and clear the buildings in the south side of the BAPAUME Road. (The remaining battalions were to take the remainder of the village and consolidate the position.)

8th East Lancs Regt. will carry out the attack. 6th Bedford Regt. will follow in support. 11th Royal Warwick Regt. will follow the 6th Bedfords. 10th Loyal North Lancs. Regt. will carry stores etc.

The Brigadier-General will meet all commanding officers at 6.30am today at Headquarters of 8th East Lancs. Brigade Headquarters will be established at this point.

On occupation of the village 111 Brigade will pass through 112 Brigade and attack the German 2nd line.

Artillery bombardment will commence at 8.20 am, and at 9.20am will rake slowly through the village. All artillery fire will be on the German 2nd line north of the Windmill by 11am.

Flares will be shown by the most advanced line of infantry at 12 noon, 4pm and 8pm.

Each battalion should endeavour to carry up a reserve of grenades in rear of it.

Further details will be given at Conference at 6.30am today.

A telephone wire will be run forward from Brigade Headquarters in the rear of the 3rd Bn by Brigade Signal Officer.

All reports to 8th East Lancs. Headquarters.

Watches should be set at 6am through the Signal Service.

(Sd) E. Stourton, Major,
Brigade Major,
112 Infantry Brigade.
Issued at 3.50am.
All Bns:
112 MG Coy.
112 TM Battery.[10]

The planning for the attack on Pozières at 9.20a.m. by 112 Brigade had partly been influenced by the alleged evacuation of the village and the differing reports from patrols about the extent of the village's defences. However, on a strategic level, the assault was an attempt by Fourth Army to consolidate the gains of 14 July's dawn attack. At 9a.m., 33rd Division would attack the Switch Line; 7th Division attempt to take High Wood and what became the infamous Battle for Delville Wood began with a thrust by the South Africans of 9th Division. On the right of 112 Brigade, 1st Division was to capture Pozières by attacking westwards from the fringes of Bazentin-le-Petit Wood. Indeed, 112 Brigade's attack was seen in the orders as a support to 1st Division's left, not the latter aiding the former's right. Meanwhile, 25th Division, on the left of 34th Division and part of a different Corps and Army, had given assurances that they too would support the attack on Pozières by attacking from the west. Everything seemed to be in place.

The Battle for Pozières – St Swithun's Day, 15 July 1916

As day dawned, a heavy mist lay over the ground, heralding a bright warm Saturday. It filled the low ground behind Contalmaison Wood as the men of the 8th Battalion East Lancashire Regiment left their trenches and formed up for the attack on the Contalmaison-La Boiselle road. The men formed into artillery formation* for the approach – single section or platoon

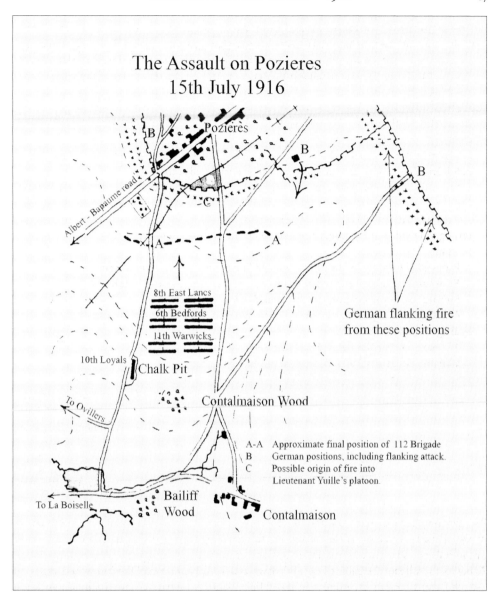

The Assault on Pozieres
15th July 1916

Pozières

B

B

B

Albert - Bapaume road

C

A   A

8th East Lancs

6th Bedfords

11th Warwicks

10th Loyals

Chalk Pit

German flanking fire
from these positions

To Ovillers

Contalmaison Wood

A-A   Approximate final position of 112 Brigade
B   German positions, including flanking attack.
C   Possible origin of fire into
            Lieutenant Yuille's platoon.

Bailiff
Wood

To La Boiselle

Contalmaison

The attack on Pozières by 112 Brigade on 15 July 1916.

files to avoid multiple casualties in the event of an artillery strike. The unit was much below strength owing to their losses of the previous few days. Yet, as this was to be their first battalion assault of the war, all ranks were keen to demonstrate that the 'Galloping Eighth' could put on a good 'show'.

In 'B' Company, Private Thomas Jackson prepared himself for battle. No doubt his thoughts dwelt at some moment that morning on his son Wilfred, living with the Reads in Burnley. Thomas Jackson was to be killed later that day, his body never recovered and he is remembered on the Thiepval Memorial. Many years later his orphaned son deposited his father's First World War letters and papers with the Liddle Collection at Leeds University for posterity, Wilfred living well into old age.

Private Thomas Jackson. Image
courtesy of the Denis Otter Collection.

At last, the battalion reached the dead ground behind Contalmaison Wood, out of sight of the enemy. Each battalion of 112 Brigade formed into company columns of platoons – two companies wide, with each company four platoons deep. The 8th were led by 'A' and 'B' companies, with 'C' and 'D' in support. The whole battalion was eight platoon waves deep and, along with the 6th Bedfords next behind and 11th Royal Warwicks following them, the whole formation was attacking on a very narrow frontage with a great depth of soldiers.

The ground itself had been heavily broken up by the British bombardment of the previous three weeks. To the north-west was the Chalk Pit, its sheer white sides cut deeply into the surrounding slopes. As the officers' whistles sounded the advance, the battalion led the brigade through the shattered tree stumps of Contalmaison Wood and then breasted the rise towards their objective.

Fifty years later, veteran Archibald Yuille remembered leading his platoon forward as a young Lieutenant. He recalled the men putting into practice what they had learned, sections advancing in short rushes, one covering the other as the platoon leapfrogged forward. Yet all the while the Germans held their fire, denying the East Lancashires an early opportunity to support the attack with covering rifle and mortar fire. Yuille recollected feeling surprised at being able to reach the top of the rise unscathed, at which point, they were met with heavy machine gun and shellfire from the village still some 500 yards distant. The German machine gunners were seen to leave their dugouts and cellars the moment the British barrage ceased. The 8th Battalion history takes up the story:

> men dropped like ninepins, and the companies rapidly dwindled away until the remnant, reinforced by other units of the brigade, managed to dig in around the Chalk Pit. Elated by their success, a large number of the enemy began to emerge from the village but were themselves driven back by machine gun fire. [11]

Lieutenant Archibald Yuille. Wounded in the attack on Pozières, he joined the RFC after recuperation. He took many of the photographs in this book with his Vest Pocket Kodak (VPK). Image courtesy of the Imperial War Museum, London. Ref. 0677/1. Also Mr Tom Yuille.

Lieutenant Yuille reached a narrow gauge railway cutting just 200 yards from the main road in Pozières. This provided good cover, though as he recalled:

> anything raised above the parapet of this cutting got a bullet in it!

The main danger for Yuille and his men came not from the front, but from the right flank, with snipers in particular picking off the men in the cutting as they fired along its length. Lieutenant Yuille was wounded in the arm in this way as he attempted to pick off one of the snipers.[12] Lieutenant-Colonel Collinson of 11th Royal Warwicks also watched the attack unfold:

> The advance up to crest had been unopposed, but as the troops came over the crest above the Chalk Pit they were met with heavy and decisive machine gun fire. This fire was so accurate that the brigade became immobilised on its narrow frontage and the three leading battalions, which had pressed forward with great boldness, became to a greater extent inter-mixed.[13]

At 10.30a.m., reports were received by III Corps that the 8th East Lancs and 6th Bedfords had reached the village and that very heavy fighting was taking place. On the brigade's right and left, it was noted by all who took part that neither 1st Division nor 25th Division were supporting the attack. The flanks of this narrow-fronted assault were in the air and the Germans took advantage. Spurred on by their success, a significant group worked its way onto 112 Brigade's right flank, causing numerous casualties, as Lieutenant Yuille had noted. The 11th Royal Warwicks withdrew one of their companies to counteract this threat. This movement caused consternation among some of the brigade, when it was rumoured that the Warwicks were retiring.[14] The company stabilised the flank, yet movement in daylight on the field was now all but impossible.

Left: Corporal John Dunn. Image courtesy of the Denis Otter Collection.

Opposite: A German sentry looks on as his comrades sleep during the Somme campaign.

Just how perilous the action was is conveyed by former Burnley ironworker Corporal John Dunn, who was in the thick of the fighting. Another of the battalion's older recruits, forty-two-year-old Dunn had been gassed and had all his teeth blown out on two previous occasions with the 8th. In a letter to his brother-in-law he explained what happened to him on 15 July:

> We went over the top at 9 o'clock. We were told to get to some shell holes about 200 yards ahead and keep the enemy engaged as much as possible, and we had to hold on at all costs, to allow our other three companies to attack a village on the left of us. I managed to get into a shell hole with four sound men, another man with a bullet through his shoulder, and another man with a bullet through his thigh, which was broken. We stuck it to 1 o'clock. I only saw one officer, and I kept in touch with him and he gave me the order to get my men back one at a time. My four men got back all right. Now this is where my trouble started. I asked the man who was wounded in the shoulder if he was going to try to get out, or he would have to stay there until dark. He said he would have a try. I helped him to the top of the shell hole. He only got about ten yards when he let go. I got a bottle of water for the fellow with the smashed thigh and then I got on the top and laid down by the side of the other fellow. He said he had got hit again. I got my equipment off and he laid on my back. I managed to get him about 100 yards with a German sniping us all the time. He got him; he was shot in the back and he rolled off me. I knew I was in for it. I lifted my head and saw a small shell hole about two yards away. I made a jump for it, but he got me all right. One of the boys saw me go down and he came out to my assistance. The fellow I was trying to get in was a stranger to me, but I found out that his name was Grimshaw. I then lay in a German dugout for five hours and then I started to walk nearly two miles to our dressing station.[15]

Corporal Dunn's war was over. His shoulder had been shattered and he had surgery to remove shrapnel from his face and nose. He won the Military Medal for his efforts in rescuing the men from the shell hole and lived to tell his four children the tale.

A great 'gathering' of men from all four battalions was to be found in the Chalk Pit, men
having become inexorably mixed. Here 112 Brigade hung on grimly, in the wood and on the
gradual slopes, under a warm sun and heavy fire. A number of battalion headquarters were
established in the Chalk Pit and at about 2p.m. Major-General Ingouville-Williams, commander
of the 34th Division, visited the scene to assess the situation for himself. He ordered a further
bombardment to take place at 5p.m. followed by another assault, calling up not only his own
artillery but also that of a neighbouring division, all available III Corps firepower and forty
large guns from the Reserve Army – 100 heavy pieces in all! The Divisional History gives a
vivid description of its effects:

> Heavy fighting in Pozières all day. This was the biggest bombardment of it, by all our heavies,
> I have ever seen. The whole place went up in brick dust, and when it was over no trace of
> a building could be seen anywhere. It was a wonderful sight, huge clouds of rose-coloured,
> brown, bluish black and white smoke rolling along together with flashes of bursts, the whole
> against a pale green blue sky and bright evening sunlight.[16]

Word passed slowly from man to man and group to group. They were to attack Pozières
once more. The signal for the advance was to be the firing of a red rocket, yet the individual
responsible for doing so mishandled its ignition, giving the Germans advance warning of the
assault.[17] Once more at 6p.m., the 8th East Lancs and the brigade advanced and once more
the German machine gunners emerged unscathed to pour a devastating fire onto them. This
came not only from the infamous Gibraltar Point blockhouse, but also west from Ovillers, still
untaken by neighbouring 25th Division. The hedges surrounding the village were thick with
uncut barbed wire and isolated parties of mixed platoons managed to reach them before being
shot down. The Lancastrians finally dug in still 200 yards short of Pozières. Their left extended
to the Bapaume Road, their right 200 yards east of the Contalmaison-Pozières Road.

Above left: Lieutenant Macqueen photographed at Foncquevillers in 1915. He was the only 8th East Lancs officer to be killed on 15 July, yet by the end of that day only three officers remained. Image courtesy of the Imperial War Museum, London. Ref. 06/77/1. Also Mr Tom Yuille.

Above right: Lance-Corporal Herbert Gavin. Image courtesy of the Denis Otter Collection.

By 8.15p.m., the action had been called off. The men lay prone and under fire until, at 2.30a.m. the following morning, those remaining were relieved under cover of darkness after seventeen hours. Stretcher-bearers cleared the wounded down Dead Man's Road, the track leading from the Chalk Pit to Casualty Corner. This advanced dressing station had been established at the small crossroads north of Bailiff Wood. The 8th Battalion East Lancashire Regiment had lost 365 casualties killed, wounded and missing. Of the eighteen officers who had taken part, only three were left unwounded. The brigade as a whole had lost 1,034 men in total.

In 'D' Company, Lance-Corporal Herbert Gavin had been killed. Twenty years of age and a former weaver from Burnley, Gavin had distinguished himself at Plymouth during basic training. He had saved a lad from drowning and had received an inscribed leather writing case in recognition of his efforts. Perhaps inspired by his gift, or presented it because he was something of a writer, Gavin had penned the following poem, which had been published in the *Burnley Express* the previous February:

> The men who stay at home at ease,
> Can go to bed just when they please,
> Have lots of 'bacca and of beer,
> But yet I'd rather be out here.
> The chaps that stay at home and dine,
> Have lots of victuals and of wine,
> With walnuts 'shelled' and all good cheer,
> But it's better to be 'shelled' out here
> The chaps who stay – the lucky dogs,

8th East Lancs soldiers on sentry duty in 1916. Image courtesy of the Imperial War Museum, London. Ref. 06/77/1. Also Mr Tom Yuille.

Can stroll about in tailored togs,
But though my make-up may be queer,
I'd rather be a scarecrow here.
The chaps who stay at home can play,
At tennis throughout the summer's day,
And ne'er fall, bleeding to the rear,
Yet it is finer to be bleeding here.

Sweethearting – oh ! You lucky chaps,
Who go a-wooing ! Well perhaps,
Unless I get a nasty scratch,
I'll get a girl when I come back.
Why yes! Who knows? There still may be,
Some girl to love a bloke like me,
There's a girl I know would shed a tear,
If I went under way out here.
The men who stay at home at ease,
May list, or enlist as they please,
For me – oh Heaven ! With conscience clear,
I much prefer to die out here.[18]

On 15 July, Gavin was missing presumed dead. His body had still not been recovered a month later and was only discovered when the battlefields were cleared after the war. He lies with several of his comrades in Pozières Military Cemetery, not far from where he fell.

The End of the Beginning

The battalion would never be the same again. Fifty-six men were known to have been killed outright, with a similar number missing. Some 250 men were wounded, many badly and some were still out on the battlefield close to the Pozières gardens. Those who made it back to 'Blighty' would later be dispersed to other battalions in the name of expediency.

During the fight, Private Peter Wakefield brought in a wounded comrade under heavy fire, having dressed the man's wounds. The award of a Military Medal for this action was widely applauded by his colleagues. Private Wakefield from Moulton, near Northwich in Cheshire, had enlisted in mid-November 1914. It had not been an easy decision, with six children to leave behind and his wife pregnant with another. Thirty-five-year-old Wakefield had been employed at Brunner Mond Chemical Works. During September of that year, nearly all men of enlistment age had joined the East Lancashire Regiment, making up two platoons of the 7th Battalion. Perhaps it was Wakefield's intention to join his former workmates. Loyalty was clearly a quality he valued, a pal reporting that he preferred to stay with his comrades than leave for medical treatment when lightly wounded early in 1916. As the friend said, 'He was made of the right stuff.'[19]

During the following month, Wakefield was recalled to his place of work to support the increase in production of nitrate of ammonia, a key ingredient of high explosives. However, he left his reserved occupation in the spring of 1918, when the manpower shortage and the German offensive of March forced many experienced soldiers back to the colours.[20] Joining 1st Battalion, Wakefield prepared for a raid one night by passing his valuables to a friend with the words 'you never know what might happen.' He was never seen again, his name recorded on the Loos Memorial.

Private John Brownlow was perhaps one of the badly wounded men brought back by Wakefield, first to the Chalk Pit, then down Dead Man's Lane to the dressing station at Casualty

Private Peter Wakefield. Image courtesy of Peter Wakefield.

Corner. He was then taken by ambulance to the main Bapaume road and driven to Heilly Station, where three casualty clearing stations on the main railway line to Amiens were situated. Brownlow, a keen amateur cricketer from Tonge Moor in Bolton, died that night. He and his brother Joe had enlisted together in October 1914 into the Loyal North Lancs before their transfer to the East Lancashires. Joe had been killed the previous December at 'Fonky'.[21]

The Learning Curve

The 8th Battalion History describes the attack on Pozières as a 'disastrous failure'. It continues:

> It was hopeless from the start: the distance to advance in the first place was too great, the artillery preparation entirely inadequate and to attempt to take the village with a single brigade merely futile. The Australians, profiting by this lesson, first of all pounded it to bits and then assaulted it with divisions.[22]

There were many factors. On 112 Brigade's left, 25th Division was still attacking Ovillers at 2.50a.m. on the morning of 15 July. Its failure meant that no substantive support could be offered, a fact that was relayed to 112 Brigade at 1a.m. Communication with 34th Division, part of a different Army Group, may have been partly to blame. As 25th Division's evaluation of the Ovillers battle makes clear:

> The Ovillers operation lacked sting on account of the absence of any definite coordinated policy … attempts being made to gain ground eastwards towards Pozières and northwards to Ovillers at the same time. The Army, Corps and Division were all strangers to each other … This lack of coordination affected the 112 Brigade attack on July 15.[23]

Second Lieutenant Blair and CSM Hall in the trenches 1916. Image courtesy of the Imperial War Museum, London. Ref. 06/77/1. Also Mr Tom Yuille.

On the right, 1st Division had 'side-stepped' eastwards during the evening of 14 July in preparation for the following day when they were to have attacked from the western edge of Bazentin-le-Petit Wood. This movement created a gap between them and 34th Division on 15 July. When the attack did take place, it was at such a distance that 112 Brigade was, de facto, unsupported.

The 1st Division had many problems of its own, resulting from poor intelligence and ineffective 'mopping up' after successful attacks. Bazentin-le-Petit Wood was still occupied by the Germans and had to be fought for until 3p.m. on 15 July! Even then, pockets of resistance in Mametz Wood took 1st Division battalions in the flank. Finally, the attempt to bomb up the old second line towards Pozières was hit hard by machine-gun fire from the village and driven back. Consequently, the difficulties of 25th and 1st Divisions left 112 Brigade to attack on a narrow front, with both flanks unsupported, as we have seen. Its head attracted a wide field of fire from Ovillers, through Pozières and from the Switch Trench north of Bazentin with deadly results. It would take the British Army some time to learn that single unsupported attacks on narrow fronts were costly and usually ended in failure.

An RFC eyewitness who saw the attack reported:

> He saw German machine gunners leave their dugouts and cellars directly the bombardment lifted. They ran down the trenches to their fire stations and opened fire at once. It appeared that the infantry had not got as close to the position as was possible during the bombardment, which gave the German machine gunners the chance of doing more damage than would have been possible had the infantry been close up.[24]

The bombardments of Pozières stopped at the allotted hour the infantry were to attack, which compounded the problem. The regular use of the creeping barrage and the adequate training of soldiers to take full advantage of it would only come to fruition in 1917. These were hard lessons to learn, a fact recognised by Brigadier-General F.M. Robinson, commanding 112 Brigade:

> The operations in which the brigade took part yesterday were, in my opinion, of the most difficult and trying nature that any troops could have been called upon to carry out. To attack a position across 1,000 yards of open country, to then remain on the battlefield from 10am to 6pm, consolidating the ground gained, under accurate machine gun and rifle fire and exposed to the enemy's artillery, and, finally, to issue from this hastily constructed position for a second assault, is a task which would try veteran troops, and which calls for the highest form of courage and tenacity. These operations were rendered still more difficult owing to the hasty preparations which the situation demanded. I am filled with admiration and respect for the officers and men who have performed this feat of arms. The losses incurred by the brigade have been serious, but a line has been secured from which new troops will be able to capture Pozières, and this brigade will have contributed largely to the capture of this place. Our conduct has won the admiration of both corps and divisional commanders.[25]

New Blood

The remnants of the battalion were relieved on 16 July. After a few days spent wandering from billet to billet, the men moved to Behencourt where the training of the specialists continued and where for ten days the survivors could find some rest and recuperation. Here, the 112 Brigade was inspected by Lieutenant-General Pulteney, GOC III Corps, who complimented all ranks on their gallantry and devotion to duty in the fighting at Pozières.

Even behind the line, men were in danger. Corporal William Parsons, an assistant at his local co-operative stores, penned letters to his parents on a daily basis. A devout Methodist who

Corporal William Parsons. Image
courtesy of the Denis Otter Collection.

regularly attended chapel and Sunday School, twenty-one-year-old Parsons went missing on
21 July. His death remained something of a mystery. The East Lancashires were marching from
Lahoussoye to Behencourt. From that day, Parsons' regular letters stopped and no more were
received by his parents at Sabden near Clitheroe. Five weeks later, they had still heard nothing
about their son and posted an appeal in the *Burnley Express* asking if anyone had heard anything
of his whereabouts. Later that week, they were shown a letter written by a friend. It said:

> I told you that Parsons has got a nice 'Blighty', but he has not been heard of since, and the idea
> was that he must have been caught by a shell while going down to the dressing station. It is
> one of the most distressing cases. No one can say anything about him after leaving the line to
> have his arm dressed, and no station or field ambulance has reported him.[26]

Corporal Parsons was officially declared dead two weeks later. The agony would go on for his
family. His name is recorded on the Thiepval Memorial.

On 26 July, 170 other ranks and seven officers were drafted into the battalion, with another
eighty-seven soldiers joining them a week later. There had been drafts before, but not on
this scale. Many of the originals who had camped at Windmill Hill had gone. The battalion
continued to rebuild throughout the autumn, supplemented by men who had enlisted under
the Derby Scheme. Some of the conscripted men called up as a result of Parliament passing
the first Military Service Act on 27 January 1916 also began to appear.

Lord Derby had been appointed Director-General of Recruiting on 5 October 1915.
His task was to make one last effort to devise a voluntary scheme of recruitment before
conscription was introduced. The Derby Scheme, as it became known, involved the canvassing
of every man between the ages of eighteen and forty-one. Each was to be asked either to
join up at once, or to attest his willingness to serve when summoned. Attested men were
split into two categories; married and single, with nineteen year olds being called up first of
all.[27] The relative failure of the Derby Scheme to boost recruitment substantially led to the

introduction of conscription early in 1916. However, the second Military Services Act passed by Parliament on 25 May 1916 had the necessary 'teeth' to ensure that an adequate supply of men was sustained into 1917. Under this legislation all single and married men between the ages of eighteen and forty-one were liable for military service, although men were not to be sent abroad until they attained the age of nineteen.[28]

Over the coming months, the battalion became host to an increasing number of South African officers. At the outset of war, South Africa, as a Dominion, rallied to Britain's side. South African troops were sent into the German protectorate of South-West Africa, but a rebellion by those Afrikaners opposed to war with Germany was only defeated in mid-1915. One soldier who was to serve with the 8th Battalion was Spencer Fleischer. Born in Johannesburg in 1892, his father had fought with the British against the Boers at the turn of the century. At the outbreak of the First World War, Fleischer enlisted in the Imperial Light Horse and took part in the South-West African campaign. As the campaign ended, he was discharged as Corporal in August 1915 and was determined to continue the fight against the Germans, perhaps believing that the best way of doing so was alongside the British, like his father before him.

Upon completing his basic training at Bedford, Spencer Fleischer joined the 3rd Battalion at Plymouth. During the autumn of 1916, he joined the 8th Battalion as a subaltern and fought with it until his transfer to the 11th Battalion in 1918, with whom he was awarded a Military Cross.

The battalion was changing its mentality also. Once the soldiers had rested and shaken off their fatigue, a new confidence came to them, having come through their first battle. In spite of the losses of friends and the ultimate failure of the attack, they had been 'blooded', fought their battle and could look the regulars in the eye.

> Between those who had been in the show and those who had not there was a gulf fixed. It may have been due to a certain delicacy on the part of the latter; but the gulf existed.[29]

Yet there was fighting enough for all and it was not long before the 8th East Lancashires were once more in action.

Bazentin-le-Petit and Goodbye to the 34th Division

At the end of July, 34th Division moved eastwards, allowing the Australian divisions to take up positions opposite Pozières. The new front ran from the western edge of High Wood to a line of trenches running east and west, and about 300 yards north of Bazentin-le-Petit. The 112 Brigade took up positions opposite to what was called Intermediate Trench. Here an interesting position prevailed, as the War Diary relates:

> In this position the left company (C Coy) shared a trench with the enemy and were separated from him by two barriers. A bombing attack was organised on the night of 7th and 8th of August with the object of capturing as much as possible of that part of the trench held by the enemy. Two bombing parties were organised under Lieutenant Burnett – one to proceed along either side of the hostile trench and bomb the enemy out. The enterprise was timed to start at 2am on the 8th. As soon as the first party tried to reach the hostile positions the enemy opened heavy machine gun fire and threw bombs vigorously. The enterprise was unsuccessful.[30]

Eighty-five further casualties were inflicted at Bazentin, though the new drafts were for the most part preserved from the bombing attacks. One exception was Private Walter Killalea, who, just prior to his death on 8 August, had had his twenty-third birthday. Killalea was one of the

Private Walter Killalea. Image courtesy of the *Blackburn Times*.

Private Harold Halstead. Image courtesy of the Denis Otter Collection.

first non-volunteer soldiers to join up and fall in battle. He had enlisted in the Army in April 1916, and had married at the same time, perhaps as a result of having been called up. Conversely, he may have wed to join the ranks of the married men and delay his conscription. Killalea had only three months' training in England, and arrived in France at the beginning of July to complete it. His death in the attack on Intermediate Trench came as his new wife and her in-laws were on holiday in Blackpool. Walter's brother had been killed on 20 June. The war was intruding with increasing brutality upon the lives of ordinary families.[31] Mysteriously, Killalea's name, like those of his comrades who fell at Bazentin, is recorded on the Arras Memorial.

On 11 August, the battalion was relieved and occupied the support trenches in Mametz Wood, where they remained for two days. Their time attached to 34th Division was at an end and, ten days later, the men rejoined the 37th Division at Dieval, in Artois. Here the unit was inspected by Major-General Count Gleichen for the last time, before his removal at the end of October. At Dieval, the ubiquitous football matches and the organization of numerous sporting events helped to create *esprit de Corps* between the 'old and 'new' men, while the officers organised mounted paper chases among themselves, to the delight of the performers and audience alike.

> The standard of Athletics at this time in the battalion was very high. Several of the subalterns were excellent 'rugger' players; we had a few members of professional 'soccer' teams and a large proportion of the men were enthusiasts at Northern Union Rugby game. Our star cricketer was Lieutenant Minaar, who had just failed to get his cap for South Africa. Lieutenant Fisher was a real 'tearer' at the quarter mile and sprints. At the brigade sports at Dieval, Fisher won the 100 yards, 220 yards and a grueling quarter mile (*sic*); almost on top of that he had to take part in a relay race, which he won for us by making up a deficit of at least a third of a lap − a wonderful performance.[32]

Training was entered into with renewed vigour and at the beginning of September, the newly reconstituted 37th Division went back into the line just south of Loos, where they remained for a month. The battalion suffered only one fatality during this time. Private Harold Halstead from Burnley was killed by shellfire on 4 October. It seemed that even those men who had come through unscathed from the Pozières attack could not lead a charmed life indefinitely, as Lieutenant Burnett pointed out to Halstead's wife:

> Your husband was killed instantaneously by a shell two days ago. In the attack on Pozières on July 15th he saved a machine gun, and it is commonly said in the company that he would have been recommended for a decoration if the company commander had not been hit. I have visited the grave, which is in a pretty spot behind the line, in the brigade cemetery. A neat cross will be placed over it.[33]

Mrs Halstead also received another letter from Private Varley who gave more information about his 'Pal's' death. The formality of the letter hints at the sadness of the ending of a friendship:

> He was in a dugout when a trench mortar dropped a shell upon it and buried both men. They were dug out as quick as possible but Harold was dead, having been killed instantly. He was buried in a soldier's grave behind the line. He was as good a 'pal' as anyone could have. I can hardly believe that he has gone, as we have been together two years.[34]

Harold Halstead, a weaver in civilian life, was a machine gunner with the battalion who had been wounded three times before his death. He left a wife and child at his Parkinson Street home in Burnley. He was laid to rest in Tranchee de Mecknes Cemetery, Aix-Noulette, ten miles north of Arras.

Towards the end of October, Lieutenant-Colonel Mackay, who had commanded the men in their first action, was replaced by Lieutenant-Colonel Webb-Bowen, fresh from the Middlesex Regiment. The periods in charge for many battalion COs on the Somme were an increasingly brief experience, as fatigue, age and ill health took their toll. In addition, tolerance of alleged inefficiencies was also lessening at all levels of command. For the 8th East Lancs and their new CO, winter was fast approaching. There was time for one last Somme offensive.

WINTER WARFARE – 1916–17

Background to the Fighting: The Ancre – November 1916

At the beginning of November 1916, the Battle of the Somme had been raging for more than four months. The Commander-in-Chief, Sir Douglas Haig, had much to consider as the heavy rains of early winter came. On 15 November he would meet with Marshal Joffre at Chantilly to agree joint plans for an offensive during the spring of 1917. The French were cock-a-hoop after making gains at Verdun during October and they would be expecting the British to keep up the pressure in Picardy.

Joffre could not countenance the arrival of German reinforcements on the Meuse, as a result of the British bringing a premature end to hostilities on their part of the front. However, Haig knew that his own troops needed to be conserved for the joint offensive in the spring.[1] He was looking for a way to strengthen the British position at the Chantilly talks when, from 8 November, the rain stopped falling, offering one last opportunity to make a significant gain on the Somme. The front-line villages of Beaumont-Hamel and Serre had successfully resisted Allied assaults since 1 July. They were to be the goal of this last offensive in 1916 – the second phase of the Battle of the Ancre. As Haig stated in his diary:

> The British position at the Chantilly meeting will be much stronger, as memories are short, if I could appear there on the top of the capture of Beaumont-Hamel, for instance and 3000 German prisoners.[2]

In addition, the Germans would not expect an attack at this time and a victory would raise spirits in Britain and hearten her allies. However, Haig was aware of the risks involved, both strategically in the field and politically at home. He also knew that the ground was deep in mud and that the River Ancre was in flood. On 31 October he wrote:

> In the afternoon I rode to HQ, Fifth Army at Toutencourt. I wanted definite information as to the state of the front-line trenches and whether the winter leather waistcoats had yet been issued, also whether an extra blanket per man had been sent up. Malcolm, General Sir Hubert Gough's Chief of Staff, assured me that everything possible was being done for the men but the mud in front is quite terrible.[3]

The newly designated Fifth Army, under the command of General Sir Hubert Gough, would carry out the assault. While the rain held off there was no time to lose. Gough decided to begin the attack

Conditions close to the River Ancre in November 1916.

on the following day – 13 November. Fifth Army had already been preparing for an assault, the primary objective being to straighten out the salient in the British line. The capture of Beaumont-Hamel, Beaucourt and Serre, along with the Redan Ridge, was at the heart of the strategy.[4]

The main responsibility for the attack fell upon Lieutenant-General E.A. Fanshawe, commander of V Corps. The 63rd, 51st, 2nd and 3rd Divisions would undertake the offensive, with the 37th Division in Reserve. This last division, including the 8th East Lancashire, was to:

> pass through the 63rd and 51st Divisions and capture a line some distance beyond the objectives of these divisions, which were Miraumont and Beaumont-Hamel respectively. Subsequent events caused this role to be entirely modified.[5]

The assault on the 13 November began from the positions used on 1 July. In between Serre and Beaumont-Hamel lay the Redan Ridge. Its capture was important because it dominated the Allied positions to the west and, if secured, would give the British an excellent vantage point over the German lines. It would also enable a flank attack to be made on Serre.

From 140 metres above the surrounding land, excellent views were to be had from the Redan Ridge. The highest part of the plateau ran about 500 yards wide on an east-west axis and then turned abruptly south in the direction of Thiepval. The keys to the German defence of the ridge were Munich and Frankfurt Trenches. These positions followed a north-south line running from their junction with Lager Alley down to the Beaumont-Beaucourt Road over a distance of approximately 1,400 yards. Running roughly parallel about 250 yards apart, Munich and Frankfurt Trenches had been heavily fortified by the Germans.

Yet it was the task of the 2nd Division to attack here on 13 November and, initially, its attacks met with success, yet faltered later on. Reserves were needed and 37th Division was to provide them, specifically 112 Brigade. Yet again the latter would not be fighting under their divisional command, but were to be attached to the 2nd Division.

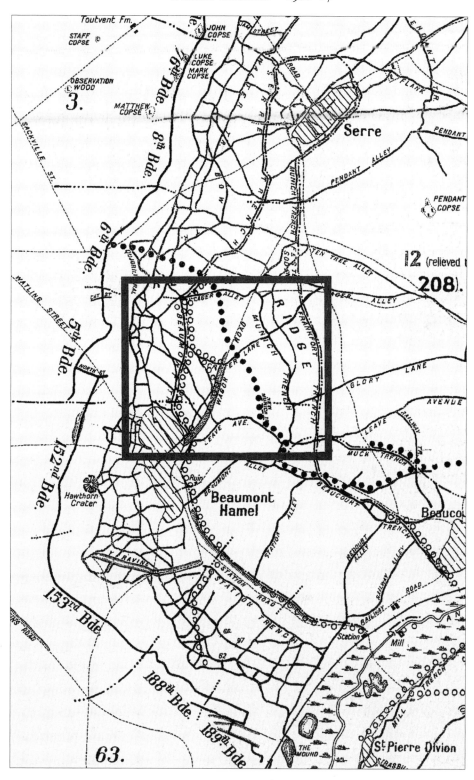

The area of the Redan Ridge. The 8th East Lancs approached from the direction of Watling Street during the early hours of 15 November 1916. Image courtesy of Fulwood Barracks.

Moving into Position

The 8th East Lancashire began to move up in support during 14 November, arriving at Mailly-Maillet at 4p.m. This village was just behind the front line of 1 July and was full of activity. Batteries of artillery were regularly situated there and the large wood to the south-west of the village was used by troops to site bivouacs. The men threw themselves down on the ground, knowing that once more they were going into battle. They would usually know by the activity around them that an attack was imminent. Orders would be given for equipment to be cleaned up, machine-gunners to check that panniers were full, signallers that their equipment was in order and that bombers had a full supply of hand grenades.[6] Predictably they faced the prospect of action in a wide variety of ways: some with jaunty confidence, many more with a thoughtful and reconciled awareness, others with unashamed loathing and apprehension.[7] Some wrote last letters to loved ones, others made out their wills, written in battered pay books.

Corporal George Mooney from Blackburn may well have had mixed feelings at the thought of going into battle. The twenty-one year old, who worked as a spinner at his local mill, had tried to enlist no fewer than ten times before being accepted the previous January. Mooney's difficulties in enlisting, perhaps because of a medical condition, or more likely his lack of height, illustrated the degree of perseverance typical of many who wanted to serve their country. He was killed the following day and laid to rest in Waggon Road Cemetery, one of the small battlefield cemeteries close to where he fell.[8]

Almost a month after the forthcoming battle, an 8th Battalion machine-gunner, Lance-Corporal William Mullen, was lying wounded in a military hospital in Leith, Edinburgh. He had been injured on 15 November and wrote home to his parents in Accrington, describing the battle:

Corporal George Mooney. Image courtesy of the *Blackburn Times*.

My dear mother and dad,

Just a few lines to let you know that I am doing fine after the effects of my wound. I am in hospital in Scotland. I was wounded on the last big push on the Ancre on the 15th of November. I will try and give you a description of the battle. As you know I am a Lewis gunner and in charge of a Lewis gun and gun team, which consists of 5 men and myself. I have had 17 months in the firing line, and as any soldier in France knows a machine gunner's work is anything but a bed of roses – a machine gunner's life is not worth the toss of a brass button once he is spotted by the enemy.

On the 14th of November we had orders to pack up. We had orders to march to a village just behind the firing line to await orders. The order came to fall in about 1am on the 15th of November. Everyone knew what that meant.[9]

This is the Chain of Command within which 8th East Lancs and 10th Loyal North Lancs operated on 15 November 1916:

Chain of Command

Fifth Army	General Sir H. Gough
'V' Corps	Lieutenant-General Sir E. A. Fanshawe.
2nd Division	Major-General W. G. Walker.
99th Brigade	Brigadier-General R. O. Kellett*
112th Brigade	Brigadier-General P.M. Robinson
10th Loyal North Lancs	Lieutenant-Colonel R.C. Cobbold
8th East Lancs.	Lieutenant-Colonel W.I. Webb-Bowen

*Kellett was in temporary charge of 112th Brigade during its attack on 15th November 1916.

The Attack on Frankfurt and Munich Trenches, Redan Ridge – 15 November 1916

Just after noon on 14 November, Major-General W.G. Walker, GOC 2nd Division, received a phone call from Lieutenant-General Fanshawe GOC V Corps. An attack was to be made on Munich and Frankfurt Trenches the following morning at 9a.m. Walker explained that the 112 Brigade had no knowledge of the ground and that, as the previous attack had been very hurried and had failed, he was afraid that if this was carried out in a hurry it would fail too. He suggested that the attack start at 1p.m. to enable the officers to see the ground in daylight. This proposal was not accepted by Fanshawe. Walker and Brigadier-General Robinson, commanding 112 Brigade, decided that the only feasible way of giving the attack a chance of success was to place the two battalions, 8th East Lancashire and 10th Loyal North Lancashire, under the orders of 99 Brigade (Brigadier-General R. O. Kellett), whose men had attacked there the previous day.[10]

Just before midnight on 14–15 November, Walker issued orders for the two battalions to rendezvous at 2a.m. at the windmill outside Mailly-Maillet. From there, Lance-Corporal Mullen described the approach to the battlefield:

We marched through endless communication trenches, and getting out of the trenches we tramped across a great many fields that were nothing but one mass of shell holes, and the mud was almost up to our waists and water over our knees in most places. I shall never forget it.

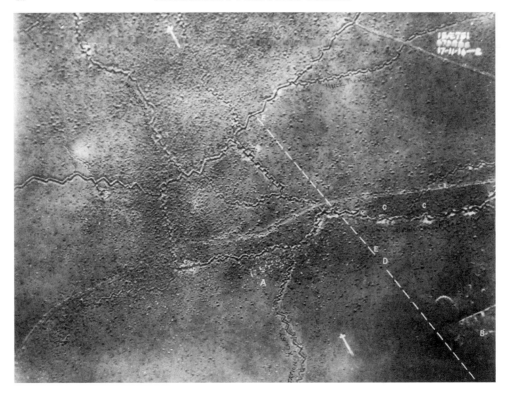

Aerial photograph of the Munich/Frankfurt trench system on 17 November 1916. Image courtesy of the Tank Museum Bovington. (TM 5086/D5)

It was bitterly cold and fritz was knocking sparks off us with shrapnel. Many men dropped exhausted through struggling to get through the mud. At last we got to our destination. Many would have taken it for a trench, but it was one continuous line of big deep shell holes. We rested here for about an hour.[11]

It was only at 7.45a.m. that the two battalions arrived in Beaumont Trench, the jumping-off point for the attack. There was not much time before zero. Beaumont Trench lay approximately 1,250 yards west of Munich Trench. The terrain covered a relatively flat area of ground in front of the East Lancashire position. Further south, it fell away towards Beaumont-Hamel. The purpose of the attack was laid out in 2nd Division Order No.166, issued at 2a.m. on 15 November and quoted here in full:

Two BNs of the 112th Brigade will attack and capture FRANKFORT TRENCH tomorrow (*sic*) between the Southern Boundary of the 2nd Divisional Area and LAGER ALLEY.

These BNs will move from MAILLY at 2am on the 15th under instructions which have been issued and will form up ready to attack at zero with their right on WAGGON ROAD.
ZERO will be at 9am on the 15th.
Field artillery will barrage MUNICH TRENCH for 6 minutes commencing intense at ZERO. This will be the signal for the infantry to get close to the barrage. The barrage will then lift 50 yards in 3 minutes till it is 150 yards beyond FRANKFORT TRENCH when it will become defensive. Both FRANKFORT and MUNICH TRENCHES must be taken with a rush as the barrage lifts off them.

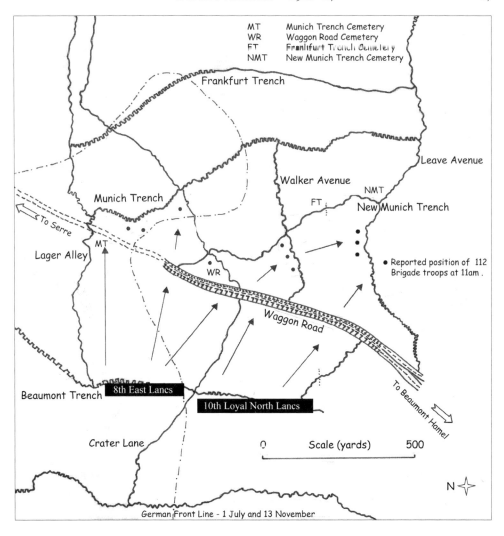

MT	Munich Trench Cemetery
WR	Waggon Road Cemetery
FT	Frankfurt Trench Cemetery
NMT	New Munich Trench Cemetery

Frankfurt Trench

Leave Avenue

Walker Avenue

NMT

Munich Trench

FT

New Munich Trench

To Serre

MT

Lager Alley

WR

• Reported position of 112 Brigade troops at 11am.

Waggon Road

To Beaumont Hamel

Beaumont Trench 8th East Lancs

10th Loyal North Lancs

Crater Lane

Scale (yards)

0   500

N

German Front Line - 1 July and 13 November

Attack of the 8th East Lancs and 10th Loyal North Lancs on Redan Ridge.

The Heavy Artillery will fire on FRANKFORT TRENCH, commencing at ZERO and lift off a few minutes before the field artillery.

The 51st Division will be attacking on the right of the 2nd Division.

The operations will be carried out under the orders of the CO 99th Brigade

Issued at 2am to all concerned.[12]

The 8th East Lancashire war diary explained that, at 8.30a.m., after the preliminary bombardment of Frankfurt and Munich Trenches, the men advanced between Crater Lane and Lager Alley in two waves. In the fog they got to within 50 yards of Munich Trench, 'A' and 'D' Companies leading the way, followed by 'B' and 'C'. Suddenly they were fired upon by machine guns and rifles at very short range. The men went to ground, yet 2nd Lieutenant Jarintzoff took a platoon into Lager Alley and captured eleven Germans, before being forced to pull back.

2nd Lieutenant Arthur Moorhouse. Image
courtesy of the Walter Holmes Collection.

Lieutenant Minaar, one of the South African officers, determined to silence an enemy Maxim,
was gunned down. The attack petered out, the men digging in across the battlefield, unsure of
where they themselves, or the enemy were. Lance-Corporal Mullen of the 8th East Lancs gave
a full account of his part in the action:

> Then the order came to fix bayonets and prepare to attack. Men fixed their bayonets, I loaded
> my Lewis gun. I might add here that my company opened the attack. I was on the left flank
> with number 3 and number 4 platoons, no 3 platoon being my own platoon. Lieutenant
> Moorhouse was in command of no 3 platoon and Lieutenant Cunliffe was in command of
> number 4 platoon. Both these officers are Accrington lads and led the men in splendid style.
> Lieutenant Moorhouse was at my side when he gave the order to us. These were his words:
> 'Come on lads and follow me!' No sooner had he given the word of command than every
> man jumped the parapet in fine style.[13]

2nd Lieutenant Arthur Moorhouse was never seen again. Public school-educated Moorhouse
was the son of middle-class parents from Leeds. In 1914, the twenty-one year old had a bright
future as a salesman with a well-known Manchester firm. Like many of his background, and at
the height of the 'Pals' recruiting, Moorhouse joined the 20th Public School Battalion of the
Royal Fusiliers.[14] Such enlistments were not universally popular:

> The middle-class and professional classes form exclusive companies, they do not hasten away
> to the nearest recruiting office, for fear they should rub shoulders with their less polished
> fellow beings. Their patriotism does not run to that.[15]

There were more practical objections to class-based recruitment. In such public school units
were many men serving in the ranks with officer potential. Moorhouse travelled to France with
his unit in October 1915, being promoted to Lance-Corporal soon after. He was then sent back

German trenches at Beaumont Hamel 1916.

to England in April 1916 for officer training, having no doubt demonstrated potential leadership qualities. After training at Bristol, Moorhouse was granted his commission the following July, joining the 8th East Lancashire early in October. Early in 1917 he was announced to be missing, presumed dead on 15 November. He is listed on the Memorial to the Missing of the Somme, at Thiepval.

Mullen's description of the attack continued:

We had not gone more than 100 yards when the Germans spotted us coming. As soon as they saw us they jumped out of the trench, planted their machine gun on the top and simply poured lead into us with a coolness and skill that any machine gunner might envy. Our lads were dropping down like skittles, but still we kept going and hung onto the enemy like glue. Most of the Germans retired into the second line as our lads got among them. We had been at it all day. We had got settled in the trench and I set my gun in readiness for any counter attack that might come. At this time LT Cunliffe asked me if I had seen any of the other officers. I replied 'No Sir.' He said if any of the men come in get them extended as far as possible in case of a counter attack. I did this as best I could as we had only a handful of men left.

About 6pm the Germans set up a terrible bombardment. It was hell and how I lived through it I do not know. About 6.30pm one of my men got killed. All the bad luck seemed to come at once. I got a terrible smash over the right eye with a lump of shrapnel. I remember seeing thousands of stars and had a buzzing noise in my head. It was a narrow escape thanks to my shrapnel helmet, which no doubt saved my life. The shrapnel went right through. My pal dressed my wound and I felt a little better. The next shell that came dropped on the gun, blowing up and wounding two men of my team. We could do no more then, so we set off for the aid post and I shall never forget my journey. I was wandering about in no-mans land for three hours and in the pitch darkness I did not know whether I was walking into the Germans' or our own trenches. I am almost sure that I was near the German line more than once. Times without number I fell into deep shell holes. In many places I could scarcely get

Private Wilfred Smith. Image courtesy of Joe Heap.

Private Harold Eastwood. Image courtesy of the Denis Otter Collection.

through the mud. I had no idea where I was. I was growing very weak from loss of blood and I knew that if I wanted to reach the aid post I would have to make a bid for it, so I decided to take one direction and risk it, wherever it lead me to. But I did not mean to let the Germans get me without a fight for it, as I was armed with a couple of bombs and my revolver was fully loaded in six chambers. But as luck would have it I had taken the right direction and arrived at the field ambulance in an exhausted condition. I met my brother Charlie at the Field Ambulance and I must give their stretcher-bearers the highest praise for they worked very hard indeed carrying in our wounded. I was put in a motor ambulance where I fell fast asleep after a hard day's work.[16]

In the foggy and featureless conditions that prevailed on the ridge that day, it was easy to lose the whereabouts of both the living and the dead. Many of the casualties were listed as missing. Private Wilfred Smith from Colne was among them. Smith was a cotton-weaver who had only come to France the previous July. Typical of many parents, his mother and father sought help from the British Red Cross. After what must have been many agonising months waiting for news, their greatest fear was realised:

Dear Madam,

We know how anxious you are for tidings of your son, Private W. Smith and we have made many enquiries for him among his comrades. It is a real disappointment to us that we have failed to obtain any information as to his fate. It is impossible that he can have been taken prisoner by the Germans, for in that case his name would long ago have reached us on the official lists which come to us from Germany.

On November 16th (*sic*) 1916, the day on which your boy was last seen, the East Lancs made an attack from Mailly-Maillet towards Beaumont-Hamel. In this attack they were exposed to very heavy fire, and though they took some trenches, they afterwards had to retire, and they lost many men that day. We have come at last to the sad conclusion that your gallant son must have been killed and buried by a shell, which as you know, throw up a great quantity of earth. We know how hard it is when the last hope is gone and we offer you our deep sympathy in your great loss.[17]

Nevertheless, Mr and Mrs Smith continued in their quest for news of their son's last moments. His identified remains are missing to this day, though he is remembered on the Thiepval Memorial.

Lieutenant-Colonel R.C. Cobbold, the commanding officer of the 10th Loyal North Lancashire Battalion, in his report of 22 November, explained what he saw that morning, making serious accusations:

My battalion formed up outside BEAUMONT TRENCH with left on CRATER TRENCH and advanced at 8.35am on a true easterly bearing, the direction by the left being taken by companies. We suffered some casualties from machine gun fire while forming up on the high ground. No casualties occurred until after reaching WAGGON ROAD, when as my right and centre emerged from the sunken WAGGON ROAD, 3 shrapnel and 1 heavy shell burst in our midst. One group was annihilated by the big shell and the company suffered heavily from the shrapnel. We still advanced suffering all the time from our light barrage till about 8.55am. The battalion arrived in a trench, mostly connected shell holes, lying 150 yards, due West and parallel to MUNICH TRENCH. We were caught by the 6 minute intense barrage behind which we retired 50 yards and reformed. We lost at this trench almost entirely from our own barrage. 8 officers were killed out of 15, 6 wounded and approx. 170 men. One of our surviving company commanders afterwards saw some Argyle and Sutherland Highlanders in LEAVE ALLEY, who had seen the whole thing and they declared that our barrage was so short that not even a splinter would have reached MUNICH TRENCH. It is contended that we ran into our intense barrage. After reforming the battalion under one of the surviving officers we again advanced, but the barrage was by then well away and MUNICH TRENCH was alive with men and machine guns. The morning was foggy.
Nov. 22 R C Cobbold BMX/57[18]

The war diary of the 8th East Lancashire accounts for the lack of progress in the attack to:

the barrage being short, the thick fog and the wire in front of the trench being uncut … The casualties during this attack were very severe, especially in officers, ten of whom were killed.[19]

Many of the East Lancashire officers killed that day had only just joined the battalion. They had been attached from other reserve units mainly in England and this was their first battle. Among them was 2nd Lieutenant Edward Fisher from London, freshly joined from 3rd Battalion. He was one of the youngest officers to die in the British Army during the First World War. He was just seventeen years old and is buried in Waggon Road Cemetery, near Beaumont Hamel.

Removing the wounded from the Redan Ridge was no easy matter and Private Harold Eastwood was one of the few evacuated to the 5th Field Ambulance, part of 2nd Division. A Burnley weaver, he was an active trade unionist, being a collector and worker on behalf of the Burnley and District Weavers' Association. Called up in the previous June, Eastwood only arrived in France two months previously. His parents were keen members of the congregational church, helping to support the Green Street Mission, and Harold, their only son, had entered the fellowship at its opening. News of his death on 17 November, from wounds suffered two days previously, caused a vote of condolence to be passed in church. Many messages of sympathy were later received by his parents from members of the closely knit congregational churches throughout Burnley. He was thirty years old and had lost his life on his first trip to the trenches. He is buried in Mailly Wood Cemetery.[20]

Neither the objective, nor Munich Trench, had been secured. The attack had been a disaster. The two battalions had lost eighteen officers between them and approximately 350 casualties overall. Lieutenant-Colonel Cobbold's allegations that his officers and men had been killed by friendly fire were to be investigated. Having been relieved the following day, 112 Brigade went into reserve in Mailly-Maillet.

More Hard Lessons

Such were the losses and the allegations made that, on 16 November, Lieutenant-General Fanshawe convened a conference at V Corps Headquarters. This meeting reviewed the operations in progress and reaffirmed the *modus operandi* of V Corps. An investigation was ordered about the attacks of the previous day. General Gough was among those who were to comment. The findings of all the reports can be summarised under the following headings:

Intelligence

There was confusion as to whether Munich Trench had been captured on 14 November. A telegram issued by V Corps and received by 2nd Division early on 15 November stated Frankfurt Trench to be the objective and made no mention of Munich Trench, implying that it was occupied by the British. For the officers of 112 Brigade, bringing forward their men in the dark at that time, there was no time to digest the subtleties of a complex and ever changing local situation.[21]

Command and Control

General Gough was critical in his report of the level of control exercised at Corps level. He believed that too much responsibility was placed upon the GOC Divisions. With respect to Munich Trench he expressed the view that:

> It would have been better to have given the attacking units a definite hour for reaching and leaving that intermediate objective. (Munich Trench) The action of artillery and infantry would then have been co-ordinated from Corps Headquarters.

Gough was also critical of the fact that neighbouring troops' jumping-off point was some 750 yards ahead of the 112 Brigade in Beaumont Trench at zero hour. He queried the part played by GOC 112 Brigade Brigadier-General Robinson, who had allowed the attack to take place under the orders of 99 Brigade. The Army commander called this 'an improper proceeding' and believed that if Robinson had kept in touch with the situation, then there was no reason why he should have handed over control of his brigade. Gough continued:

> There seems to have been no reason why the battalion and company commanders should not have gone ahead leaving the battalions to be brought on by the adjutant. Troops must realise that they cannot have days for reconnaissance. We must act quickly sometimes; but to enable us to do so commanders must exercise foresight.[22]

Spare materials used to maintain the 8th East Lancashire trenches, 1916. Image courtesy of the Imperial War Museum, London. Ref. 06/77/1. Also Mr Tom Yuille.

However, both Fanshawe and Walker believed that it was only by giving command of the two 112 Brigade battalions to 99 Brigade that the attack stood any chance of success. Nevertheless, by 1 December Robinson had been removed from his post.

The Infantry's Involvement

The size of the force employed in the attack was also questioned in General Gough's report. He queried why only two battalions were available for the attack. Fanshawe countered that 99 Brigade had been used up in the attacks on the 14 November.[23]

Walker was clear that the attack had been carried out in too much of a hurry and that the men lost direction owing to the fact that forming-up places had not been taped parallel to the objective. He explained that the officer of the right battalion (10th Loyals), who was directing the attack by compass, was killed shortly after leaving Beaumont Trench:

> and although the order was given to the men to keep their right shoulders up, the direction was too much to the right. The lie of Wagon Road and the direction of Crater Lane also tended to deflect troops to the SE instead of the E.[24]

Captain Dyson of the RFA was clear that the East Lancs and Loyals had lost direction and had gone too far to the right.

> I saw a number of their officers ... They said that they had suffered casualties from our barrage, but fully realised that this was because their left had advanced too quickly and swung to the right ... Some of their officers to whom I spoke were under the impression that they were in Munich Trench (Instead of Walker Trench {Avenue}).

In other words, facing at right angles to their correct line of attack! As a neighbouring unit reported.

> The attack failed to reach its objective, the men advancing too rapidly and being caught in our own barrage. The troops of the 2nd Division on our left lost direction in the mist and swung to the right across our rear in a very disorganised state.

The Artillery's Involvement

General Gough stated that the orders issued by V Corps to the artillery were not clear. More significantly he questioned why fifty yard lifts were ordered for the entire barrage. No doubt Walker and Kellett wished to slow the movement of the barrage when their troops were moving over difficult ground. Walker also believed that the troops got too close to the wire because of the difficulty of recognising the ground and the misty conditions. The result was that when the barrage began at zero some of it came on the infantry. Consequentially, the men retired back, while the barrage began to creep forward, giving the Germans time to reoccupy Munich Trench in strength. Captain Sloan of the RFA spoke to officers wounded during the attack:

> When our barrage increased at 8.20am, the infantry thought we were then bombarding Munich Trench and when our fire increased intense at 9am they thought the barrage was lifting and they walked straight into Munich Trench. Some Companies lost direction and turned south and the German artillery shooting from Puisieux caught them in their backs and they probably thought it was our artillery.[25,26]

The seriousness of what happened on 15 November was further illustrated by the fact that, on 30 November, an independently observed test shooting of six batteries of 2nd Division artillery was ordered. The results of the test were said to be satisfactory, with no shells being recorded as falling short. It added, however, that the artillery's task of providing an accurate barrage on Munich Trench had been difficult because the ranges were long, observation was difficult in the preliminary registration of the targets and the wind and temperature were constantly changing.

On 28 November Brigadier-General Kellett, GOC 99 Brigade, submitted a paper entitled 'Lessons learnt during operations 13/17th November 1916'. The paper made clear how the Army was trying to learn from its mistakes, many applying to the attack on 15 November:[27]

> The necessity for Divisional and Brigade Staffs taking steps to know the positions of both friendly and enemy troops continuously throughout an action was important. Staff officers were to be active in seeking out this information. Brigadiers were to know exactly where their flanks rested and whether there were any gaps in the line. Kellett made clear the importance of allowing plenty of time for getting orders to the lower formations if a fresh operation was to be undertaken. Also, that attacks should be so timed as to allow the objectives to be reached in broad daylight. He felt that landmarks previously explained to units might then be recognised.
>
> Taping a line parallel to the objective was imperative. Troops were to be given not only the definite objective, but also the compass bearing of the general line of advance. Officers were to be ready to make an advance or attack at short notice. Reconnaissance was to be made without delay and officers should act without waiting for orders. Kellett had found that an intelligence party, having no other work than the collection of information, was very effective in this role. All entrances to enemy dugouts were to be secured and sufficient men were to be left behind to 'mop up' the defenders.

The importance of keeping close to the creeping barrage was reiterated. It was only as men became exhausted and the barrage got away that casualties increased significantly. During the attack on 15 November 50-yard lifts every three minutes had been agreed to enable the men to keep up with the barrage in the heavy going. In such conditions the rifles' breech mechanisms failed and the extractors broke. Men's hands became so filthy that Kellett suggested that the troops keep their rifle covers on and only take them off when they arrive at the first objective.

What Happened to the 8th East Lancashire on 15 November 1916?

From all the accounts, it is possible to gain an understanding of what happened to the 8th East Lancs on 15 November, their second disastrous assault four months to the day since the ill-fated Pozières attack. This assault suffered from a lack of preparation. There was not time for officers to grasp the details of the orders, nor was there time for the troops to observe their objective and get to know the front over which the attack was to take place. The men were exhausted after a five-hour march through atrocious conditions, in the dark. One of the primary reasons for tactical failures throughout the course of the war was later analysed as follows:

> 'decision-making on the hoof' was almost always disastrous. Yet it was a bad habit which persisted well into 1917, leading to attacks that were called at too short a notice and on too narrow frontages, before essential preparations could possibly have been made.[28]

The conditions under which the attack took place contributed to its failure.

> Churned up by shell fire and turned into a morass by constant rain, rapid advance was impossible and the men were knee-deep and sometimes thigh-deep in mud.[29]

Poor visibility and the troops' lack of knowledge of the ground led to complete confusion.

The East Lancs was bombarded by 2nd Division's artillery as the result of the men not being able to identify Munich Trench. The short artillery lifts may well have contributed to the difficulties and men were hampered moving over ground churned up by their own artillery. Observing the movement of the barrage must have been difficult in the mist, especially if the initial bombardment was thin and as the creeping barrages carried out at this time consisted solely of shrapnel shells. Indeed, there were two more alleged incidents involving 2nd Division artillery and 'friendly-fire' on 18 November.

> The principal reasons for this failing were worn guns, defective ammunition and inaccurate location of the infantry forward positions.[30]

The British Army was trying to learn from the setbacks and high casualty rates of the Somme Campaign. The investigations carried out following the assault of 15 November were typical of the gathering of evidence from lower formations and units in the summer and autumn of 1916.[31] Nevertheless, they were brutal lessons to learn.

The End of the Battle of the Ancre

On 17 November, the 37th Division relieved other divisions within the Corps, holding the front line from the Ancre itself up to Beaumont-Hamel. The latter village had been captured on 13 November, but Serre and the Redan Ridge remained in enemy hands. No further assaults were made, merely small advances undertaken to straighten the line. The 8th East Lancs were completely done in. For the next four days time was spent in open shelters, or in occupation of deep dugouts in the old German line where a brigade could easily be accommodated, and there was a bakery, a hospital and even a soda factory! Comparisons were made between these defences and those occupied by the British. Yet as an eyewitness recounted, above ground the conditions in the German defences were appalling:

> Shells were tearing over our heads and crashing into the station thirty yards away. We clung to the side of the bank, picking our feet delicately between the debris of a Bosche Wagon team, bones, blood and guts of horses, the heads with ghastly staring oyster eyes. Above this shambles hung the stench of blood and the strong sweet odour of an apple loft, the smell of gas.
>
> In this muddy wilderness where every natural and human feature had either been blotted out or twisted to an unrecognisable form, and when the attempt to recognise those features could only be made through the blackness of a November night, through an atmosphere whipped with bullets and torn by explosion. Where to leave the known plunged the seeker in ten paces into the unknown, and sent him perhaps blundering into a nest of Germans, no man could be blamed for inexactness in plotting points on a map.[32]

On 25 November the battalion was relieved and by the end of the month was under canvas in the tiny village of Val de Maison. The snow began to fall, which, combined with hard frosts, conspired to make the men's rest period even harder than usual. The 7th East Lancs Quartermaster was called in

A cheerful member of the battalion in the trenches in 1916. Image courtesy of the Imperial War Museum, London. Ref. 06/77/1. Also Mr Tom Yuille.

to make the conditions a little more bearable for his fellow Lancastrians. Eventually, more substantial billets were found at Beauval, where the men stayed until mid December, when the influence of the new commander of 37th Division was felt for the first time. From 14 to 18 December Major-General Bruce-Williams ordered continuous route marches to be carried out by all units, as they transferred from Fifth Army to First, changing billets each night. The Quartermaster-General recorded the distance marched each day by the battalions, and included details of those soldiers who needed to be carried and those who fell out on the way. On 14 December, the 8th East Lancs marched sixteen miles, with nine men being carried and twenty-eight falling out. By the end of the five days, in which fifty-seven miles were covered, proportionally more men were completing the distance, no doubt to the relief of their senior officer Lieutenant–Colonel Webb-Bowen. The process of retraining and hardening the men had already began.

Into the Line at Festubert

Christmas 1916 found the battalion holding the front line, this time at Festubert, in Artois. Soon after their arrival, the hardest frost in living memory descended on the Western Front, rendering doubly destructive the shrapnel and shells as they struck the frozen ground. At this time, there was one more significant change in the command structure. Brigadier-General Maclachlan took over command of 112 Brigade. Following the closing down of the Somme battle, the opportunity had been taken to re-evaluate not only strategy and tactics on the battlefield, but also to ensure that the personnel who would lead the men into battle were of the right calibre. Maclachlan's appointment completed the change in 37th Division's senior officers. All those with the rank of Lieutenant-Colonel and above, who had fought at Pozières just six months earlier, had been replaced.

Major-General Bruce-Williams inspected the battalion for the first time at Locon. He was impressed with what he found, both in the steadiness of the men on parade and their

Private Leonard Newland. Image courtesy of the Denis Otter Collection.

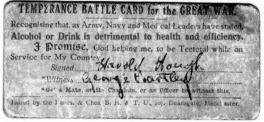

A temperance pledge card carried by Private Harold Hough of 7th East Lancs. The temperance movements had many adherents in the Army, including a significant number in the 8th East Lancs. Image courtesy of David Hough.

general turnout. This provided a welcome boost for the soldiers after their recent setbacks and Lieutenant-Colonel Webb-Bowen gave the battalion his own nickname – 'The Locon Guards'. There were also more tangible benefits from the successful inspection:

> For some time after this the battalion could do no wrong. Obstacles which had hitherto continually irritated us mysteriously disappeared; indents which had been held up weeks suddenly came through and everyone felt at peace with the world.[33]

The familiar trench routine resumed at the outbreak of the New Year. Casualties were relatively light, though the list of those killed continued to grow in the grim frozen conditions.

Private Leonard Newland was part of a working party in the front line, when he was hit by machine-gun fire in the body and killed on 10 January. Twenty-four-year-old Newland was part of the Wesleyan community in his native Burnley, a member of the young men's class of the Sunday School. He was also involved in the Temperance movement, holding the office of 'Chief Ruler' of the local 'Tent' of the Rechabites Friendly Society, representing the town at national conferences.

The International Order of Rechabites took their name from the eponymous biblical tribe who were 'commanded to drink no wine' by their leader Jonadab, son of Recab, and successfully resisted when tempted to do so. Taking their inspiration from the story, the founders of the order opened their first 'Tent', or branch, in Salford on 25 August 1835.

Newland may have found it hard to adapt to life in an organisation that had always been hard-drinking. However, he would have identified with the strong thread of religious non-conformity and temperance running through the Army. Though those that carried temperance pledge cards were never more than a respectable minority, they were sometimes mocked as 'tea busters' or 'bun wallahs'.[34] His officer, Lieutenant Haywood, may have had the recent route marches in mind when he wrote to Newland's parents:

> He was a fine little chap, always cheerful and most willing to carry out any duty to help his senior officers. Although troubled with tender feet he refused to fall out on route marches, thus setting a fine example to his fellow soldiers.[35]

He is buried at Le Touret Military Cemetery.

On 17 January, Captain Burnett's company was holding the front-line trenches, which were for the most part a series of disconnected outposts. Burnett asked men in pairs to patrol between these outposts to ensure that the areas between were clear of the enemy and that the flanks were secure. On one such patrol, Private Albert Proctor and another comrade became lost in the darkness. The battalion war diary continued ominously:

2 Other Ranks while patrolling between the islands were missing and believed to have been taken prisoners, cries being heard of 'East Lancs' and 'Mother' from towards the German lines.[36]

Bearing this in mind, Captain Burnett wrote as discreetly as he could to Proctor's wife:

He must have lost his way for presently his voice was heard from close to the German wire and one or two shots were heard. We have heard nothing since of either of these two men, but we hope that they may both be prisoners, perhaps wounded prisoners. I do not want to raise your hopes unduly, but I would advise you not to despair for another month. If you do get good news from Germany, I shall be very grateful if you will let me know. Your husband was in no way to blame for losing his way, as the path was very hard to find, the night extraordinarily dark and we had only been for a very short time in that part of the line. He was an extremely good man, who was always chosen for any important work such as being one of the guard at Brigade Headquarters. In the trenches I used him during the last two tours of duty to do the work of an NCO, and he did so extremely well that I decided to promote him immediately we went out of the trenches. He is a great loss to the company, and I hope most heartily that you will get good news before long.[37]

But there was no good news and the body of the twenty-four-year-old father of four, who worked at Towneley Colliery in Burnley, was never found. He is remembered on the Loos Memorial.

During late December and early January 1917, many of the East Lancashire men were sent on leave, taking advantage of the lull in fighting between offensives and the freezing weather that made significant action difficult on both sides of no man's land. After 1916, leave became more systematic, given by strict rotation. In theory, a soldier could expect to return home on leave once a year if he survived in France, though a man sent home wounded who returned to the front would recommence his 'year' when once more in the line. Length of leave varied from three to ten days and did not take into account any distance that a soldier might have to travel

Private Albert Proctor. Image courtesy of the Denis Otter Collection.

to get home, or the time taken to get there. Later on in the war regulations were introduced that decreed that a man's leave didn't begin until at their home line station.[38]

The rank and file were carried away in a large bus, which appeared to start in the middle of the night. This conveyance, after cruising about through various villages, picking up its quota of passengers, and waking up at the same time everyone within a mile of it, transferred its freight at some wayside station to a long, heavily laden train. The latter, which maintained an average speed of about a mile an hour, varied by long halts and much whistling, was calculated to reach its destination in sufficient time to allow passengers to be marched to some camp to wait for some other boat than the one just missed![39]

As a consequence, a short leave was of no use to a man from the North-West of England, for example. Unsurprisingly, many men took an extra day, worrying about the consequences of such actions when returned to France, to be able to pass a few more precious hours in Blighty.

As January turned to February, the harsh freezing weather continued. A rumour circulated at this time that the battalion was being pulled out of the line to form part of a special reserve. According to the speculation, the Germans were planning an assault against the Belgians over the normally sodden but presently icy areas of the line that covered their front. Rumours and superstitions usually took root because men were starved of information about their present and knew nothing of the future. Most rumours were not of the strategic type described above, but varied from the banal – what was for tea, when the post would arrive etc – to the macabre – that the occupants of a particular dugout were prone to be unlucky; or that the man who rang the gas gong was always ill-fated!

Loos Sector

On 9 February, the 37th Division relieved the 24th in the Loos sector. The Loos battlefield lay immediately north of the mining town of Lens, in the heart of the industrial area of north-eastern France. The ground here was unvaryingly flat, dominated by slagheaps, pit heads and *corons** connected with the coalmining in the district. By 1917, the various mining villages, collieries and other industrial buildings presented a difficult challenge for any would-be attacker.

The front line opposite the East Lancashire trenches ran slightly down to the bottom of the Loos valley. Mining had left a great scar across it in the form of two long ash strips running east to west. This 'Double-Crassier', found on the extreme right of the battalion front, was held by the British on its western end and the Germans at the other. Light railways, which carried coal trucks filled with slag, ran along the crest of the two mounds. At fifteen metres high, the 'Double-Crassier' provided both sides with the possibility to dominate the area around and there was regular and intense fighting to gain control of it.[40] Snipers were regularly positioned there. The 8th East Lancs defended the slag heap with a special platoon, though sometimes its main task was to protect those staff officers who found that it offered an excellent view of the enemy line, in spite of the latter's close proximity.

Since the Battle of Loos in September and October 1915, the Germans had made their part of the line almost impregnable, defended by thick razor wire, numerous machine guns and many heavy trench mortars, which were perfectly sited in the industrial landscape. In places, the opposing lines were close together or ran through ruined buildings or mine-workings, and there were numerous large craters. Many saps were pushed out into no man's land and it was perfect ground for bombers and snipers. Some said that it was the worst sector in which to serve anywhere on the British front.

On 10 February, the battalion was billeted in Les Brèbis, a small settlement behind the front line, in the rear of the southern Maroc area of Grenay. All the villages close to the front were in

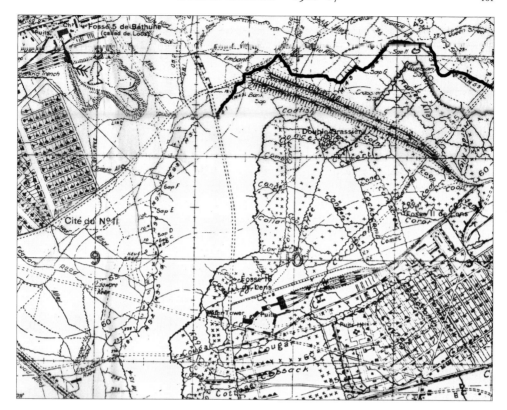

The front-line trenches held by the 8th East Lancs during February 1917 at Maroc, close to Loos, are indicated by the bold black line. The complexity of the trench systems on both sides of no man's land is evident, as are the miners' cottages, pit head no. 5, and of course the great Double-Crassier slag heap. Image courtesy of Fulwood Barracks.

ruins by 1917, the men being billeted in cellars. The next night, they went into the trenches for the first time. They were greeted with heavy shelling of all calibres and Private Milton Holgate from Sabden in the Ribble Valley was killed instantly.

A Methodist committee member of his local Weavers' Union branch, Holgate had only been conscripted the previous October and sent to the front in the New Year. He was secretary to the Sunday School and also carried out administrative duties to the Band of Hope, a Temperance organisation for working-class children. All members took a pledge of total abstinence and were taught the 'evils of drink'. Thirty-year-old Milton Holgate also found time for poultry-rearing and gardening, winning many prizes at Sabden's horticultural shows.[41]

Another Sabden soldier, Private James Holliday, wrote pitifully to Holgate's widow and child, explaining about the circumstances of his comrade's death:

I am very sorry to inform you, as I thought it my duty, that your husband, Pte. Milton Holgate No 34462 East Lancashire Regiment has been killed in action on February 11th. You must not worry yourself much, for he had a peaceful death. We buried him in the British cemetery in France, so you will know he is in a nice grave, for I went myself to see it. We were all very sorry to lose him, for we were all together. I and John Hodkinson got off lucky. Milton Holgate is buried in the Maroc British Cemetery.[42]

The Double-Crassier slag heap close to Loos. Image courtesy of Paul Reed.

Also buried at Maroc is a man from a completely different background. He was killed the following night by another intense bombardment. Lance-Corporal Edgar Hartley had been a teacher at Bradley Council School before enlisting the previous May. After recovering from a bout of influenza, Hartley had returned to duty not long before being killed. The twenty-six year old was a committee member of Nelson Liberal club, where he was renowned as an excellent player of billiards. Married with a young daughter, Hartley's wife was also a teacher at the same school in Nelson, which was close to their home in Fountain Street. As an assistant master it seemed that he was showing great promise in his chosen profession:

> He was trained at Westminster, and during his association with Nelson Education Authority he gave many evidences of becoming a most competent master. He was thorough in all that he did, and he enjoyed an unusual degree of popularity with the children at school. He was a young man of ideas and ideals and the news of his death came with a very great shock to his colleagues. He was a winning personality, and all who knew him deplore his death. He appeared to have a life of promise and usefulness before him, but the war, as in so many other instances, has cut it short.[43]

The following Easter, the headmaster of the school unveiled an enlarged photograph of Lance-Corporal Hartley, subscribed for by the staff and children. Before leaving for their holiday, all the pupils marched past the picture at the salute, in recognition of their teacher.

Captain Beattie wrote telling Mrs Hartley that her husband had died twenty minutes after being hit and was conscious to the last. Beattie, who had written many such letters, was nevertheless moved to say exclusively that:

LOOS-EN-GOHELLE. - Vue générale de la Cité N° 5, des Mines de Béthune.

A Loos pithead before the war. Surrounded by the corons – miners' cottages – this mine was just behind the 8th East Lancs' right flank.

We were very sorry to lose such a splendid fellow out of the company … He was always so smart and keen on his work, and different from the other men. I have missed him more than any other man.[44]

The tour of duty came to an end on 17 February, when the Lancastrians were relieved by the 11th Royal Warwickshire. After a seven day tour, one of the latter's officers, Captain Simms, described the conditions in that part of the line that his men would hold in rotation with 8th East Lancs:

owing to the thaw the trenches are beginning to get into a very bad state, particularly as repair work and no digging have been possible during the prolonged frost. On the second day there was a little rain and it was impossible to cope with the mud and sludge which was practically up to our knees and icy cold. It was particularly difficult for us as the support. Companies have to do all the carrying for the front line and this in gum boots, which in many cases do not fit, or even keep out the water is bound to play havoc with the men's feet. During the whole tour of six days, men's feet were rubbed with whale oil and socks changed twice daily, which means that this was going on continuously throughout the day. In spite of all the precautions we have had to report a comparatively high number of trench foot cases. The trenches began to fall in as the thaw penetrated and simply wading along a trench was sufficient to cause quite considerable landslides every few yards.[45]

Simms described the relief of his battalion:

Nearly twelve hours later, the leading platoons of the 8th East Lancashire arrived in an absolutely exhausted condition, many of them without boots. They had been forced to wait till dark and set out on the top as it was a physical impossibility to get the men, heavily loaded

Above: Private Milton Holgate. Image courtesy of the Denis Otter Collection.

Right: Lance-Corporal Edgar Hartley. Image courtesy of Fulwood Barracks.

in gum boots through the mud. One platoon had come about a third of the way down the (communication) trench, during which the men had lost their boots in the mud. It has decidedly been the most exhausting tour of the trenches I have ever had.

So bad were the conditions that this tour lasted only three days, before the East Lancs were withdrawn into brigade reserve. The men were formed into working parties, shoring up trench walls, bringing forward supplies and materials and repairing the barbed wire. In the Loos sector, wiring was often done at night, for fear of sniping from the slag heaps, although at any time of day it was an awful job. One veteran remembered:

It were the lousiest job in the world, were the barbed wire job. We went out in the pitch dark on our bellies and white tape was handed out to the man in front, and this white tape was let out wherever you went. No man's land was full of shell holes and in winter it got wet and anyone falling in had had it. Handling the stuff, barbed wire, it were terrible. The wire had inch long needles and you daren't get clipped to it because you couldn't pull yourself off, it was like someone grabbing hold of you. We wore gloves of course; just ordinary thick gloves, but you got some terrible, awful scratches. It was a terrible job at night, it was a feared job with the troops, but nobody ever refused as far as I know.[46]

Left: Lance-Sergeant John Barker.

Below: An 8th East Lancs wiring party working on the Corps Line defences close to Souastre in 1916. Their casual air and clothing indicates their position of safety relative to the front line. Image courtesy of the Imperial War Museum, London. Ref. 0677/1. Also Mr Tom Yuille.

The last man to die before the battalion left the Loos area for a prolonged period of training was Lance-Sergeant Jack Barker, from Barnton in Cheshire. At the outbreak of war he was employed in the production of glue with the Weaver Refining Company. When, in mid-November 1914, the East Lancashires were once again recruiting in nearby Northwich, Jack went with his friend Fred Norrey to join up. Fred, who lived four doors away from the Barkers, was also twenty-three. He had attended the same school and worked as a farm labourer. When the harvest was gathered in, the two hoped that they were going to join their many Barnton friends who had been recruited for the 7th East Lancs. Almost two platoons were formed from the local Brunner Mond chemical works in early September 1914. It was not to be. Jack Barker was promoted to Lance-Corporal in early 1916, full Corporal soon after the attack at Pozières and Lance-Sergeant after the assault on the Redan Ridge. He went on leave early in 1917, bathing in the tin bath in the back yard on his arrival home, while his mother removed his lousy and filthy kit. His commanding officer took up the story in a letter to his parents:

> It was on the night of February 27th that I took your son to erect wire entanglements. We had just reached the place where we were to do the work, when a machine gun opened fire, and most unfortunately a bullet struck your son just below the heart. The stretcher-bearers were on the spot, but could do little for him.[47]

He too is buried in the Maroc British Cemetery, the last in a row of 8th Battalion soldiers.

A year after his death the family placed a few words in the local paper, lines which might have stood for many:

> Sleep on, dear Jack, in a soldier's grave.
> A grave we shall never see,
> But as long as life and memory last,
> 　We shall remember thee.

Ever remembered by his mother, father, sisters and brothers, 96 Church Road, Barnton.

SPRING OFFENSIVES:
ARRAS – 1917

Turning Point

The onset of 1917 saw many significant changes in the conduct of the war. Those who had been charged with the responsibilities in the first two years found that their time had run out. In Britain, Lloyd George replaced Herbert Asquith as Prime Minister, while in France Joffre had been replaced as commander-in-chief of the French forces by General Robert Nivelle. Russia, in the grip of revolutionary turmoil, was on the point of pulling out, while America declared itself ready to fight.

Germany too had been evaluating its position on the Western Front. Its resources, both material and human, had been severely depleted during the Somme campaign. The German High Command had built a strong defensive position that its troops could pull back to should it be necessary. This new defensive trench system enabled the Germans to shorten their line, thereby making a great saving in manpower that could be employed elsewhere. While the forces of the Entente could not afford to surrender a yard of French or Belgian soil to the 'boche', the latter could relinquish ground in favour of improving their position. This new line was built even more carefully than before; on the best reverse slopes, behind huge belts of barbed wire fifty feet thick. It comprised deep ditches and ferro-concrete blockhouses connected by tunnels. Originally the position was a mile deep, consisting of three defensive lines, though this was later strengthened. During late February and early March 1917, Allied units on their usual reconnaissance found that the enemy had gone, withdrawn back to their new position, what the Germans called the Siegfried Stellung and the British called the Hindenburg Line.

General Nivelle, the hero of Verdun who had recaptured Fort Douaumont, offered a new vision of the future. No longer would the waste and slaughter of the Joffre years be tolerated. In their place, Nivelle promised rapid victories on the Western Front, won by surprise and deep creeping barrages to overwhelm the German defences. The British were to play a supporting and diversionary role. They were to attack at Arras early in April, in order to draw German reserves from the point of the French thrust later in the month in the Soissons-Rheims area.

New Methods of War

After a week spent in the relative comfort and safety of billets in the town of Bethune, the 8th East Lancs marched to Rebruviette, a short distance west of Arras to train for the forthcoming attack. From 9 to 31 March the battalion undertook:

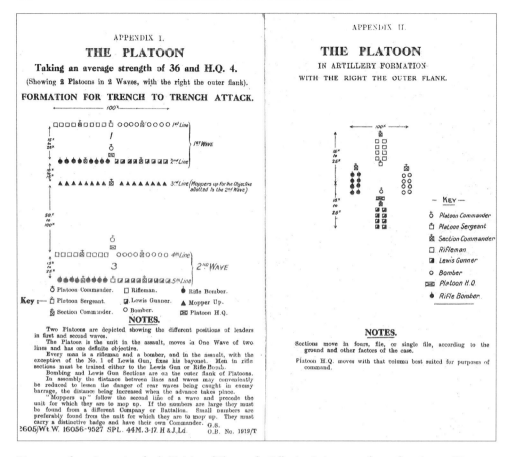

Two pages from *Instructions for the Training of Platoons for Offensive Action 1917*, often referred to as *SS143*. Image courtesy of Fulwood Barracks.

training daily and practising formation for the attack. Weather very wet and training made difficult. Practice Trenches at LIENCOURT were allocated to the battalion on Different dates. (*sic*)[1]

The formations for which the men were trained were quite different to those used during their attacks the previous year. The winter of 1916–17 saw the production of a military manual that would change the way that warfare at a tactical level would be waged. In many ways *SS143, Instructions for the Training of Platoons for Offensive Action 1917*, laid the foundation for the way in which the infantry would fight in the modern era. Rather than a solid line of riflemen the new manual placed emphasis on:

> The platoon being a self contained unit, which is divided into a small platoon HQ plus four fighting sections, each with its own speciality. The first section has three expert bomb throwers and their accomplices, the second has a Lewis gun and nine servants, the third has nine riflemen including a sniper, while the fourth section has a battery of four rifle grenades manned by a further nine men.[2]

In simple terms the attack was to be led forward by the bomber and rifle sections, with the rifle grenade and Lewis gun sections following close behind. Upon contact with the enemy, the rifles and the bombers were to seek out the enemy flank and attack with fire, bayonet and bomb. The rifle grenadiers and Lewis gun team were to attempt to suppress the enemy, allowing the other sections to press home their attack. At the heart of the guidelines laid out in SS143 was a belief that the advantages of each weapon type could be brought to bear on the enemy as and when needed. This flexible use of arms also passed a degree of initiative to the junior officers down the chain of command. In order to encourage these developments, the training regime followed by the 8th East Lancs was based upon the following requirements:

The Offensive Spirit. All ranks must be taught that their aim and object is to come to close quarters with the enemy as quickly as possible so as to be able to use the bayonet. This must become a second nature.

Initiative. The matter of control by even company leaders on the battlefield is now so difficult that the smaller formations i.e. platoon and section commanders must be trained to take the initiative, without waiting for orders.

Confidence in Weapons, necessitating a high standard of skill at arms.

Co-operation of Weapons is essential on the battlefield and the corollary of (c).

Discipline is most necessary at all times, and particularly on the battlefield.

Moral (sic) must be heightened by every possible means; confidence in leaders and weapons goes a long way towards it.

Esprit de Corps. True soldierly spirit must be built up in sections and platoons. Each section should consider itself the best section in the platoon, and each platoon the best in the battalion.[3]

112 Brigade Efficiency Competition – March 1917

	Transport	Shooting	Bombing	Bayonet Fighting	Musketry	Lewis Gun	Boxing	Relay Race	Road Race	Stretcher-bearers	Tug of war	Inter-Company	Inter-Battalion	Points Total
6th Bedfords	3	3		2	3	2	3	3	3	3	3	3	3	34
11th Warwicks	2	2	1	3	1	3		3	2			2		19
10th Loyals	1		2		2		6						2	13
8th East Lancs			3	1			2							6
Trench Mortar Battery							1							1

One of the ways of fostering esprit de corps was through competition and during the March training schedule a 112 Brigade Efficiency Competition was organised. The competition was also geared towards the development of weapon skills outlined in SS143. As the table above makes clear, however, the 8th East Lancs did not perform well, winning only the bombing competition, while the Bedfordshires dominated proceedings.[4]

One of the reasons for this may have been yet another change of command in the battalion, for on 13 March Lieutenant Webb-Bowen left to command elsewhere, his place being taken by Major Campbell, the second-in-command. Campbell would see the battalion through to the end of its war service. Good leadership was the key to the development of the efficiencies outlined in the new training manual. Following its large officer casualties in the previous November and the continuous changing of its CO, it may not be far from the truth to say that the battalion was in need of a firm, consistent approach. The poor showing in the Efficiency Competition may also have been a reflection of low numbers in the battalion, the lack of fully trained NCOs and the quantity, quality and state of training of the newly conscripted soldiers. Whatever the reasons, it is of great credit to the newly promoted Lieutenant-Colonel Campbell and his men that, by the time the Lancastrians went into battle at Arras a month later, the battalion performed creditably.

Monchy-le-Preux

> Two miles off, over the undulating grassy country and beyond the Brown Line, could be seen a village crowning the summit of a circular hill, with its red roofed cottages peeping out from among the green foliage of trees – altogether a very picturesque view. The village was Monchy our objective. There is something fascinating about the first sight – from a distance at least – of a position one has to capture; it makes one conjecture about the future, if it does nothing else.[5]

Monchy-le-Preux was one of the keys to the northern end of the Hindenburg Line. Standing upon a spur of ground below the southern bank of the River Scarpe, it dominated the five miles of ground due east of the city of Arras. The Monchy-le-Preux position gave the Germans ideal observation over the line of the British advance. Although the German line was stretched in April 1917, their soldiers still held the pre-Hindenburg trench system between the village and the city. There were four lines of defence in all, each given its own code name by the British: the Black Line – a mile from Arras; the Blue Line – 1,000 yards further east; the Brown Line – built on the slopes of Orange Hill – two miles from Monchy and finally the Green Line, just to the east of the village itself.

View of Monchy-le-Preux taken from beside the Arras-Cambrai road, on what the British called Chapel Hill. Monchy is on the hill on the left. The 8th East Lancs attacked with their right on the main road as they advanced towards their objective south of the village during 10–11 April 1917.

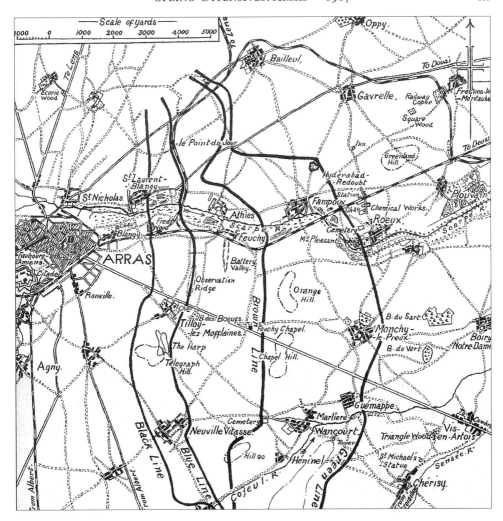

Map illustrating the places in which the 8th East Lancs fought during the battles of Arras during April and May 1917. Image courtesy of the Royal Green Jackets Museum.

The importance of capturing Monchy was made clear in the Third Army Orders. Its commander, General Sir Edmund Allenby, specified that one of Third Army's first tasks was to seize the high ground around Monchy-le-Preux and the village itself by the end of the first day. This would be no mean feat, as the settlement itself had been reinforced by a series of interlinked concrete shelters.[6] The 8th East Lancs and the 37th Division were part of VI Corps, within Third Army. The division was once more in reserve, its objective being to pass through the leading divisions, which were to attack on 9 April, and capture Monchy-le Preux and the Green Line. The objective of 9 April, Easter Sunday 1917, was nothing if not ambitious. An advance in one day to an objective five miles away, would be unprecedented on the Western Front since 1914.

The First Battle of the Scarpe – The Attack on Monchy-le-Preux, 9–12 April 1917

In the early hours of Easter Sunday, the 8th East Lancs, under their new GOC Lieutenant-Colonel Campbell, marched through the streets of Arras in heavy rain. Other units used the tunnels under the city, but the battalion, soaked to the skin, breakfasted in the open until the sun appeared about 9a.m. and made their way to the old British front line. By early afternoon, it was reported that other divisions had captured the Black, Blue and Brown Lines and the 112 Brigade was sent forward to its jumping-off point. From a track about 500 yards west of the Brown Line, with their right on the Arras-Cambrai Road, the battalion advanced towards Monchy in artillery formation. Their objective was a section of the Green Line, south of the village. It was approaching 7p.m. The men crested the lower slopes expecting no resistance from the German third line. Unfortunately, the intelligence that its defences had been taken was faulty and the men came under sustained machine-gun fire. The companies opened out into extended order, rushing from shell hole to shell hole, digging in just short of the Brown Line. At 8p.m., Captain Edmondson of 'A' Company arranged his men into two bombing groups, supporting them with Lewis guns and riflemen. The bombing groups were to look for weaknesses in the enemy positions while the rifles and Lewis guns offered covering fire. Although the attack was ultimately not successful, it is clear that Edmondson was putting the training outlined in SS143 into practice.

The men fell back onto their starting position. Soon after dark, snow began to fall and a heavy carpet quickly covered the hardening ground. The temperature dropped below freezing and a savage blizzard lashed the troops as they huddled together for warmth. There was to be no sleep and some died from exhaustion and exposure. Many with frostbitten feet had to be evacuated from the line in the morning. An eyewitness who was out that night described it as the worst he ever experienced:

Lieutenant Moses Forman photographed in 1916. One of the battalion's South African officers, Forman had completed an MA at Glasgow University before the war, joining the OTC there. He was badly wounded in the attack on Monchy-le-Preux on 10 April, dying the next day. Image courtesy of the Imperial War Museum, London. Ref. 06/77/1. Also Mr Tom Yuille.

Private Albert McNulty. Image courtesy of the Denis Otter Collection.

Private Rennie Graham. Image courtesy of the Denis Otter Collection.

> I didn't care what happened to me and as I walked along the top of the trench in the dark of the night, my eyes caught two of our men lying in a shell hole who had been killed that day. There they lay, partly covered in a thin layer of snow.[7]

Casualties had been mercifully light in the 8th Battalion and they and the rest of the division were withdrawn to the Blue Line, while the Brown Line was securely taken by other troops. Yet there was to be no respite. The 37th Division was called forward and at 1.30p.m. on 10 April ordered to capture the Green Line and Monchy-le-Preux. Scouts were pushed forward before the advance of the battalion and the 6th Bedfordshire crossed the rise of the Brown Line. The Official History described the attack:

> The brigade's action was such as could not, for smoothness and promptitude, have been excelled on manoeuvres. The 8/East Lancashire and 6/Bedfordshire were away over Chapel Hill in artillery formation before the enemy could bring down a barrage to check them. Eight guns of the 112th Machine Gun Company hastily installed on Chapel and Orange Hills at once began to barrage Guemappe and Monchy over their heads. The enemy's fire soon forced the two battalions to deploy (from artillery formation* into company waves), but the East Lancashire pressed on …[8]

Hit during the advance was Private Albert McNulty from Padiham. A conscript who had enlisted in the previous October, twenty-seven-year-old McNulty worked as an assistant at the Padiham Co-operative Society. His administrative skills were in much demand for, in addition to being assistant secretary at his local Methodist Sunday School and a keen footballer, he found time to be secretary to the Corinthians Club and the Padiham Lads FC.[9]

Private Rennie Graham, McNulty's brother-in-law, was with him when he died, the former informing his sister about her husband's death. The two men had worked together at the Padiham co-op, Graham as a fruit salesman. He was one of the battalion's footballers, who had played half-back with Padiham Lads FC. Shortly after his death later that month, his comrades received a food parcel from his wife intended for her husband, which they consumed, as was customary. One of them wrote:

> Just a few lines in answer to your parcel. We shared the same among the boys of his team. I am sorry to send you news concerning the death of your husband. He was one of my best pals. In fact he was one of our football team, and all the boys in the company are sorry to lose him, for he was so well liked.[10]

Both McNulty and Graham, who had enlisted together on 20 October 1916, were married, each with a child. Private McNulty is buried at Houdain Lane Cemetery, Tilloy-Les-Mofflaines, not far from where he fell. Rennie Graham died of his wounds received just prior to his death on 28 April. He has no known grave and is remembered on the Arras Memorial. It may have been a little comfort to the men's wives to know that they had enlisted, served and died close together.

Veteran Thomas Heap of the 8th East Lancs remembered the attack many years later:

> When we went over, one of my pals who was a veteran and had been over before said he was scared stiff and did not think he was coming back. He didn't! He was by my side when he was machine gunned, he just gasped and dropped. I stayed with him to make him comfortable. He died and I had to carry on. By the time we dug in again we had fewer than twenty men and all the officers and NCOs were casualties.

The enemy fire was growing stronger now, forcing the Lancastrians to advance with short rushes. Monchy was in the distance to the left and to the right was the Arras-Cambrai Road, a useful guide in maintaining the direction of the attack. Directly ahead, the Germans could be seen digging trenches and had 4.2in howitzers firing salvoes at close range. The 8th East Lancs also had to deal with enemy snipers who had pushed forward beyond their own lines. On the road, Les Fosses Farm and its cellars were taken in brutal hand-to-hand combat. The attack came to a halt caused by enfilading fire from Monchy-le-Preux. The East Lancs reached a line approximately 600 yards from their objective in the Green line, about 1,000 yards south-south-east of Monchy.

The falling snow now turned to a blizzard, enabling another advance by the Lancastrians at 8p.m., with 200 further yards being taken. Reports reached the battalion that 111 Brigade had entered Monchy, but had later been repulsed. No further movement was possible owing to the violence of the short-range artillery fire into 112 Brigade. The evening of 10 April was again freezing, but the men received rations brought up under fire from the rear. They were exhausted, cold and hungry, with no sign yet of relief after approximately thirty-six hours in the field and two advances under fire. One hundred men had been casualties in the battle so far.

One of them was Sergeant Mellor, a man typical of the many professional soldiers and reservists who stiffened the ranks of many New Army Battalions. Born in Salford in 1885, Mellor had joined the Army aged fourteen, becoming a member of the Corps of Drums with the East Lancashire Regiment. At the age of sixteen he was in South Africa during the Boer War. After a tour of duty in Ireland, he married a local Dublin girl in 1905, yet four years later he moved to Sheffield, first with the Police, then working with a steel firm. At the outbreak of war, Samuel Mellor rejoined 1st East Lancs from the Army Reserve, fighting at Mons, Ypres and at the Somme, where he had been wounded twice. After convalescence and retraining, he was sent to the 8th Battalion early in 1917. Returning with him was CSM Fleming, who had been wounded at Hannescamps in June 1916. Fleming wrote to Mrs Mellor almost a week after her husband's death on behalf of his company:

Sergeant Samuel Mellor. Image
courtesy of the Mellor Family.

16.4.17
Dear Mrs Mellor,

I am writing you on behalf of the Officers, NCOs and men of D Coy to try to express to you our deep and sincere sympathy with you and your children in the loss of your dear husband. Your loss is ours also, for he was a gallant and fearless soldier and a particular favourite in the battalion and thoroughly liked and respected by everyone for his cheery ways and good spirits. He was killed on the 10th of the month whilst the Batt. was attacking the enemy and he was leading his Platoon and cheering them on when he was hit and he suffered no pain for he died immediately. I am very sorry that we cannot send you anything belonging to him for the man who went to his aid is missing and he removed his personal effects. I can fully realise what a great blow his death will be to you for I was with him at Plymouth and we came out together and I think I knew him better than most men and I had a great liking and respect for him, for his unvarying cheerfulness, straightforward honesty, and above all he was one of the finest soldiers I ever met. In conclusion we hope and pray that God will soothe and comfort you and your children in your hour of trial and help you to bear your great loss.

I am yours respectfully.

CSM Fleming of D Coy 8th East Lancs.

Another NCO in 'D' Company, Sergeant Gawthorpe, wrote to her the following September. The high degree of esteem in which Mellor was held by his comrades was clear:

A dead German machine-gunner left in the ruins after the capture of Monchy-le-Preux.

Dear Mrs Mellor,

Thanks for your letter safely received, also thanks in anticipation of the photo of dear old Sam. Well Mrs Mellor I think the last letter I sent you must have gone with a lot more to the bottom of the channel, however, I am very sorry to tell you I have no hope of ever getting you your dear husband's treasures, as Sergt. Major Fleming has since been wounded and is now in England.
I really don't know who the man was you refer to in your letter as (*sic*) been missing, because there was an awful lot of poor fellows who we shall really never know what happened to, but in order to do my best for you I have found out that dear old Sam was buried very nice at a place called Monchy le Preau (*sic*) in front of Arras and a cross is there to mark the spot, hoping this will be a great satisfaction to you and your family.

The grave was later lost, however, and Sergeant Mellor is commemorated on the Arras Memorial to the missing.

The Capture of Monchy-le-Preux – 11 April 1917

There was to be no respite yet for the battalion. At just after 5a.m. in the morning, Major-General Bruce-Williams ordered 37th Division to resume the attack on Monchy, where 111 Brigade were to capture the village itself while 112 Brigade were to capture Green Line, just east of the Monchy-La Bergère Road. The two brigades were to keep in touch throughout the advance. 8th East Lancs were to follow 10th Loyals and 11th Royal Warwicks to the objective.

The weather was worsening, snow falling heavily as the dawn came up, and was blown into drifts by the freezing wind. The men moved forward, immediately under heavy fire from Monchy, some of the enemy machine guns located in trees, to cover the dead ground into which the 112 Brigade came as they approached the village. Immediately to their front a tank of 'C' Battalion, 1 Tank Brigade advanced, giving momentum to the battalions, as they passed the windmill on the Monchy-La Bergère Road. Private Ernie Wilford of 11th Royal Warwicks remembered his part in the attack:

> It was so cold that morning that we took our boots off stuffed them with straw and set fire to it. Then we put our feet in 'em. That was the only warmth we got. Well, the attack went in, and we got no briefing at all. I hadn't got a clue where I was going. That was the trouble, you never knew what you were supposed to be doing. I seemed to be harnessed in a mob. Where the mob went, I went – just follow the crowd … like sheep really. Well right from the start I threw my pack away. It was too heavy and what with slipping in the slush I didn't care less. Then I saw it – you wouldn't believe it, just on the left of the Arras-Cambrai Road, long lines of men just mowed down, lying flat where they went forward.[11]

Facing the attack of the 112 Brigade was Musketier Herman Keyser of the 84th Reserve Regiment:

A romanticised version of the capture of Monchy-le-Preux, typical of the work of the artist and illustrator Frank Dadd.

A stylised representation of the use of cavalry during the First Battle of Arras by David Bell.

It was dawn when the call came, 'The Tommies are coming!' and without any covering fire they advanced in lines up the Arras-Cambrai road. We were lying about 150 metres to the left of it, and there was a tank supporting their attack and when it was directly opposite our trench the thing started shooting at us with eight machine guns. Our rifle fire was useless against it and we had to withdraw. Later we saw the tank burning on the hill.[12]

Meanwhile, to the north, elements of 111 Brigade had entered the village itself, where there was fierce fighting. The 8th East Lancs reached their objective in the Green Line, while some elements pressed 200 yards further on. Others held positions south of the road in the direction of Guémappe.

By 9a.m., the village had been taken, yet between the two brigades a gap had opened up, exposing the flanks of both to counterattacks. This was filled by the arrival of units of 3rd Cavalry Division, which had been on the battlefield since the previous day, awaiting the possibility of a breakthrough that they could exploit. Some cavalry regiments charged into the village and at the retreating Germans. 3rd Dragoon Guards dismounted and took up firing positions next to the Lancastrians. The war correspondent of *The Times*, Philip Gibb, described their appearance:

You have never seen cavalry like them – mud encrusted figures in flat metal hats, men with three days' beards and faces covered with grime in no way suggesting the smart Lancers, Dragoons or Hussars of other days. They had slept in shell holes or lain in mud and rain with no protection save their greatcoats.[13]

The Dragoons, with their Hotchkiss machine guns, had arrived just in time. The Germans counter-attacked twice that evening. They brought up aeroplanes, shooting up the horses and

British cavalry Hotchkiss machine-gun teams gallop into action close to Monchy-le-Preux.

directing artillery fire down on to the line. Only one East Lancs officer was left in all four companies and reinforcements were sent down from the HQ at Tilloy.

Sergeant Baker from Bury was awarded the Distinguished Conduct Medal during the action, as the citation awarded for his actions illustrated:

> He was the only sergeant left in his company; he took charge and reached the objective, which was held after repulsing two counter-attacks. Throughout he showed great initiative and personal courage, setting a fine example.[14]

This was not the last that was to be heard of Sergeant Baker.

By 9p.m. and with Monchy in British hands the battle came to an end. All around the East Lancashires were the bodies of almost 200 horses and the bodies of dead and dying cavalrymen. Looking back from the 1980s, ex-Private Thomas Heap of the 8th East Lancs remembered one of the last charges ever undertaken by British cavalry:

> It was here that I had witnessed a tragedy. I watched a cavalry charge moving up from Arras into the village. They were massacred, there were horses and riders falling all over the place and very few survived.

Although the majority of 112 Brigade troops were in positions south of Monchy village, a few individuals had been swept up into the village itself, or went there later that evening. Private Edgar Crane of 6th Bedfordshire was one of them who found warmth and food. In one house he discovered sausage, bread and tinned chicken, but it was still a dangerous place to be:

> We all went down the cellar to get stuck into some grub, while our Lance-Corporal, a nice chap who was due to go on leave the next day, kept watch at the top of the steps. Suddenly he came rolling down the steps into the cellar. He had been shot dead. That spoiled our appetites.[15]

British troops boarding London omnibuses at Arras on their return from the capture of Monchy-le-Preux by men of the 37th Division, 11 April 1917. (This image also appears on the front cover of this book). Image courtesy of the Imperial War Museum, London. Ref. Q6228.

Later that night the whole of 37th Division was withdrawn. Guy Chapman, returning from leave, witnessed the infantry returning to Arras along the main road:

> On the left infantry were coming back, dirty, unshaved, their tattered clothes white with chalk and grey with mud, their faces sallow with exhaustion. They shuffled blindly along in single file, their eyes on the ground. They passed and staggered on the uneven pavé. They never turned when a hurrying ambulance hooted behind them, but lurched heavily to the side. They never looked up; they were too tired even to face this wan light. Each was a lonely secretive figure, its mind turned inward, desperately drawing the shrivelled soul back to life.[16]

The capture of Monchy-le Preux was made notable by the Army and the British press as a great breakthrough – five miles of ground taken in just three days. From now on however, German resistance would stiffen at Arras.

The Second Battle of the Scarpe –The attacks on Greenland Hill, 23–28 April 1917

General Nivelle's long awaited attack on the Aisne took place on 16 April. There was no breakthrough in forty-eight hours as he had promised and the French Army went onto the defensive, caused by heavy losses. Morale fell at all levels of command and there were mutinies in many of the regiments. Even before Nivelle was sacked in the middle of May, the Germans could concentrate all their forces on the British at Arras.

Second Lieutenant Bertram Fawcett on the left, with a fellow officer early in 1916. Rising to the rank of Captain, he was killed leading his company in the battles for Greenland Hill, close to the village of Gavrelle. Image courtesy of the Imperial War Museum, London. Ref. 0677/1. Also Mr Tom Yuille.

The Lancastrians' time was now spent cleaning up, resting and training behind the line once more. The battalion took no part in working parties during the ten days out of the line, a sign of the degree of the men's fatigue. Nevertheless, 37th Division was transferred back to the trenches on 22 April. This time, they took up positions roughly three miles due north of Monchy-le-Preux and a mile south of Gavrelle. They were opposite Greenland Hill, the capture of which was the division's objective. About a mile due south of the East Lancashire positions was the village of Roeux. Gavrelle, Roeux and Greenland Hill, on the northern side of the River Scarpe, were all in German hands. On 9 April they had been in a position that equated to Monchy in the German defences i.e. the Green Line. Now they formed one of the last lines of defence, holding the key to the high ground and the partially constructed sections of the Hindenburg line beyond.

112 Brigade was in divisional reserve on 23 April, when the main assault took place in the early morning. During the day, the men were moved forward towards Greenland Hill to support the attack if necessary and the Germans put down a barrage of high explosives and shrapnel. As the battalion reached Hussar Trench, an explosion lightly wounded Lieutenant-Colonel Campbell and seriously injured the Adjutant Captain Parks and the officer commanding 'D' Company, Captain Fawcett. Parks was evacuated to England, spending the remainder of the war in hospital in Kent. He never recovered from his wounds, dying in August 1919 at the age of twenty-four.

Bertram James Acton Fawcett was twenty-four years old. His father was a retired Indian Army Colonel and the family were from Blackheath in London. Educated at Cheltenham College, he was a good athlete who had a talent for cricket, as the Cheltonian Society Magazine described:

BJA Fawcett. Distinctly the best bat on the side; is a left hander with a very strong defence and plenty of shots on the leg side. He makes his off strokes very well but without sufficient

Private Arthur Wilson. Image courtesy
of the Denis Otter Collection.

force to get past the fielders on the slow wickets that prevailed. A very fair catch, but slow on
his feet.

In 1910, he went to Ceylon, where he founded his own business at the age of eighteen! He played
cricket regularly for the city's cricket team, taking on Victor Trumper's Australians two years later.
He left the sub-continent in October 1914, obtaining his commission the following month. He
embarked with the 8th East Lancs for France and, aside from three short leaves, saw continuous
service with the battalion. He was Mentioned in Despatches shortly after his death on 22 May. As
one of the battalion's original officers his loss was keenly felt, especially having come through the
battles for Monchy unscathed. He is buried at Aubigny Communal Cemetery Extension, which
served two casualty clearing stations ten miles north-west of Arras.[17]

The battalion, already seriously weakened, was about to go into action scarcely 200 strong
and with key officers missing. At 4.15p.m., Colonel Campbell received the order to attack
Greenland Hill. The men moved forward in the open to Chilli Trench, part of the Black Line.
The men were instructed to keep close to the barrage and at zero hour the diluted companies
moved off. As they passed the Gavrelle-Roeux road they were hit hard by flanking machine-
gun fire from the infamous chemical works close to Roeux, sustaining heavy casualties as they
went. In addition, German planes strafed the head of the advance and had to be driven off with
Lewis guns.[18] The men dug in just beyond Cuba Trench, capturing an advance German mortar
position in the process.

Badly wounded in the attack was nineteen-year-old Private Arthur Wilson from Burnley.
In the absence of any news that he was in hospital, his parents told the local paper that they
presumed that he had died in the field the following day, on his way to the casualty clearing
station. He was buried in the small cemetery at Haute-Avesnes, nine miles west of Arras. Wilson
had enlisted as a seventeen year old in March 1915, but had not been sent abroad because of his
age. In some cases where underage men enlisted and their age became apparent, they were sent

Private Walter Evans. Image courtesy
of the Denis Otter Collection.

back home and called up at the appropriate time, or, as in Wilson's case, remained in a training
battalion to prepare him for the front. During his time with the reserve he had become a Lewis
gun instructor and offered promotion, which he had declined. Prior to war, he had been a
weaver and before that was a member of his school's swimming team. Private Wilson had been
born at Clinton, Massachusetts, but his family had returned to England when Arthur was two
years old to resume their lives in their former home town.[19]

The German position that had done so much damage to the East Lancashires was 'The
Chemical Works', a derelict dye factory made up of old vat houses, engine sheds and chimney
stacks that had been fortified. The Germans had occupied it with many machine guns and
snipers and it was connected to a huge blockhouse nearby with a series of tunnels. The position
overlooked the whole plain to the west and north. The attack on 'The Chemical Works' during
the morning of 23 April by a neighbouring division had failed, enabling the machine gunners
to enfilade all of the British attacks to their north, in the direction of Gavrelle.[20]

Another victim of the enfilading fire from 'The Chemical Works' was Private Walter Evans,
at first pronounced wounded and then missing. Twenty-three-year-old Evans was married with
one child, born soon after his departure for France in August 1916. The family lived in the *Tim
Bobbin Hotel* in Burnley, though whether Walter worked there is not clear. It may have been
that the family had come in search of work in the Lancashire area and were living at the hotel
temporarily, for Walter and his wife had come from Birmingham, where he had been actively
involved with the Oddfellows Institute.

The Oddfellows began in the City of London in the late 17th and early 18th centuries
and established local groups across England and Wales. This growth was spurred on by the
Industrial Revolution – as people began to stream into towns and cities to work the need for
mutual protection was soon apparent, at a time when there was no welfare state, NHS, personal
insurance or even trade unions. Only by joining mutual friendly societies like the Oddfellows
could ordinary people protect themselves and their families against illness, injury or death.

Private Miles Fawcett. Image courtesy
of the Denis Otter Collection.

Indeed, when the Asquith government was setting up the National Insurance Act in 1911, it
used Oddfellows' records to work out the level of contributions.

The connection with the society may have been important to Mrs Evans, for not long after
Walter had departed for France, their child died. One can only guess at her state of mind and
circumstances after the death of her husband. His body was recovered after the war and he rests
at Point-Du-Jour Military Cemetery, Athies, at a cemetery used to inter all those previously
'missing' from the nearby battlefield.[21]

Lieutenant-Colonel Campbell was ordered to Brigade HQ on 24 April for treatment to his
wounds.[22] The remnants of the battalion were put under the command of Major Courtney
who pulled them back to the Black Line, where the men rested during the next three days.

During the afternoon of 27 April, Major Courtney met with two of his surviving officers
to make the arrangements for one final push towards Greenland Hill. 37th Division was to
capture the lower slopes, the battalion playing a supportive role to the 10th Loyal North
Lancs. The fact that two companies were to be led by relatively junior officers illustrated
the diminished state of the battalion. Second Lieutenant Speak was to lead the whole of
'C' and 'D' Companies and 2nd Lieutenant Cunliffe 'A' and 'B'. These two soldiers were
the last of the experienced officers capable of leading the men in action. There were others
recently arrived from the latest draft, but Courtney needed men familiar with battle, on
whom he could rely.

One last time and greatly under-strength, the 8th East Lancs moved forward towards Greenland
Hill at 4.25a.m. on 28 April. The assault began well, the men reaching Cuba Trench with few
casualties. Lieutenant Frank Speak gave orders for 'D' Company to consolidate this trench under
a junior officer while he took 'C' forward to the objective close to Cuthbert Trench. Here the
company was hit by fire, not from their front, but again from 'The Chemical Works', which was
earning itself an evil reputation among the British troops. Speak pushed on beyond Cuthbert
Trench but was wounded in the process. So intense was the fire from the south that he was

pinned down and could not move back, nor could his men reach him over ground. Instead, the men of 'C' Company formed a defensive flank facing south in an old communication trench between Cuthbert and Cuba Trenches. They returned fire into 'The Chemical Works', while some dug a short trench out to 2nd Lieutenant Speak, who was later able to report back to Battalion HQ. What remained of the battalion consolidated the communication trench facing south, as the flank was in the air and exposed to potential counter-attacks. The Germans duly obliged and were in turn met with devastating artillery fire:

> They came crawling over the top of Greenland Hill in three lines, about six hundred strong. They were just starting down the forward slope when something flashed in front of them. A column of bright terra-cotta smoke was flung upwards … Another and another rose until an arcade of smoking pillars seemed to move across the hill-side. 'Six-inch How,' shouted my neighbour excitedly, 'firing one-o-six'. The first line was hardly there. It merged with the second and mechanically the whole inclined southwards to avoid the shells. But the guns followed the movement and another line of smoking columns fountained into the air. At last reduced to one line, the minute figures turned and stumbled back over the crest of the hill.[23]

During the action, one of the officers ordered Private Harold Blezzard to relay a message to Major Courtney at the Battalion HQ. Leaving his comrades on the lower slopes of Greenland Hill, Blezzard made his way slowly back approximately 500 yards, through the fire of the Maxims, to the jumping-off point for the attack. Later that afternoon he made the reverse journey, carrying a message to the forward companies. He was awarded the Military Medal for his efforts, returning home to a hero's reception at the Burnley Palace, where he was presented with the decoration by the mayor in front of a large and enthusiastic audience. Twenty-one-year-old Blezzard joined the Machine Gun Corps in 1918, ultimately receiving his medal on 31 August that year. He survived the war.

During the last six days, the battalion lost close to 200 men. Over forty had been killed on 28 April alone, many from 'C' Company, which had borne the brunt of the attack. Their bodies were left close to the German line. As the East Lancs were relieved the following day there was no time to bring in the bodies of the fallen. As a result, many of the men killed opposite Greenland Hill have no known grave and are commemorated on the Arras Memorial.

Among them was one of the NCOs, who were important to the battalion operating efficiently in battle when there were so few experienced officers to call upon. The wife of Sergeant Fred Holgate from Rawtenstall received a letter from one of the battalion's officers:

> Dear Madam,
> It is with great sorrow that I write to tell you that your husband was killed in the attack on Saturday April 28th. He was slightly wounded on the 23rd, but like the great hearted man that he was, remained on duty, and on Saturday he was killed by a bullet through the head.
> Your husband reached the rank of sergeant more quickly that any man I ever met. I was so much impressed by the value of his work in the affair at Beaumont-Hamel in November, that I marked him for speedy promotion. His untiring energy and never failing cheerfulness were wonderful to see.
> I never can forget the last night we stood in the trenches. After a week of misery and cold, we expected to be relieved and at the last moment we heard that we had to stand another night there. I detailed your husband for the most unpleasant job, that of taking a series of shell holes, 300 yards in front of the lines and he got his party together so cheerfully that one would have thought he enjoyed the work.
> He would certainly have got the DCM for his work in the last show if he had not been killed, but unfortunately the VC is the only decoration given to the dead. I shall recommend him very

strongly for mention in despatches as one of the finest men and finest soldiers that I ever met. But so few names are mentioned in despatches that I cannot be sure that anything will come of it. You have my most sincere sympathy in your terrible loss, which has been a great blow to me also.[24]

Also killed was Private Miles Fawcett, a bookkeeper and assistant foreman at the bottle works in Burnley. A practicing Wesleyan, Private Fawcett, like many men of his generation, used his professional skills out of work, acting as secretary for providing lectures to the Accrington Co-operative Newsroom. Newsrooms had developed during Victorian times and were often related to libraries to:

> propagate instruction and useful information, create a taste for reading, promote the formation of good behaviour and form an excellent competition against public houses and other objectionable pastimes.[25]

Private Fawcett left a wife and two children. His name is remembered on the Arras Memorial.

The battalion was relieved that night and taken back to Arras in buses once more. The Second Battle of the Scarpe was over. The struggle to reach and overcome the defences of the Hindenburg Line would continue in the Arras theatre for several weeks.

Return to Monchy – The Attack on Hook Trench, 31 May 1917

The Third Battle of the Scarpe was fought on 3 May, with the intention of attempting to break out into open country between Monchy and the Hindenburg Line. The attack failed miserably along most of the front and the Battle of Arras was officially closed down two weeks later. Yet fighting continued in the vicinity of Monchy until the end of the month, when the British turned their attention to the Messines sector. It was to be on the last day of May that the 8th East Lancs went into action once more.

Throughout the first half of May, the battalion rested in the village of Ambrines, west of Arras. Some officers and men were evacuated back to the UK with sickness, while drafts arrived in large numbers to bring the unit back up to strength. By now the number of those men who had joined the original battalion at Codford was very few. It was mostly made up of conscripted men and those who had been wounded in earlier battles and returned to the front.

Ominously, the battalion began to practise night manoeuvres and brigade strength attacks on 10 May. It seemed that there was to be very little respite from the offensives opposite Arras. The men moved back into the line on the night of 20–21 May, this time south-east of Monchy, the line having moved very little in their absence. Two days later, they undertook salvage operations in their immediate vicinity, retrieving precious rifles and other detritus of war that could be reused. There were dead to be buried too, some of the corpses having been out in the open since the middle of April. The effect of this work on nineteen-year-old recruits was recalled by one veteran, over eighty years later:

> The flesh had mainly gone from the face but the hair had still grown the beard to some extent. They looked very ragged, and the rats were running out of their chests. The rats were getting out of the rain of course, because the cloth over the rib cage made a very nice nest and when you touched a body the rats just poured out of the front. A dozen bodies would be touched simultaneously and there were rats tumbling everywhere. To a rat it was just a nest, but to think that a human being provided a nest for a rat was a pretty dreadful feeling. And when the flesh goes from under a puttee there is just a bone and if you stand on it, it just squashes. For

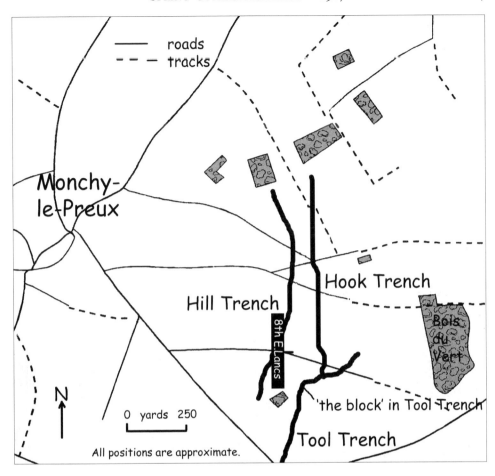

The attack on Hook Trench at the end of May 1917 was the battalion's final action in the Arras Campaign.

a young fellow like myself, nineteen, all I had to look forward to at the time was a similar fate. It still has an effect on me now, you never forget it.[26]

Some of the trenches held by the East Lancashire were just north of the Arras-Cambrai Road, south-east of Monchy, while others were in old German line across the road. The left company held part of Tool Trench, an old communication route into the German line. The eastern end of this trench was still held by the latter and there was a constant bombing exchange to gain the initiative. Nevertheless, the stay was a brief one and the battalion was relieved on 25 May. There were rumours that the division was being withdrawn for further rest and training and that the enemy were retiring. Yet, a few days later, the battalion was informed that it was to be attached to 29th Division for a night assault on Hook Trench! How this news was received is not recorded, but one can guess the soldiers' reactions. On the afternoon of 27 May, the men were given baths after practising attacks on dummy trenches at nearby Tilloy.

Hook Trench lined the forward fringes of Infantry Hill and VI Corps gave instructions to 29th Division that it be captured by 31 May. Hook Trench would provide a position to launch a further attack on the Bois du Vert, the highest point around and from where the German artillery observers directed artillery fire from beyond the Hindenburg Line. 8th East Lancs were placed under the command of 86 Brigade on 29 May. The attack was scheduled for the night of

One of the unburied dead.

29–30 May, but was cancelled at the last minute when a soldier from one of the neighbouring battalions went missing and was feared captured. The element of surprise was considered key to the success of the attack, which was postponed for one night, though zero hour and other details were changed. Yet, as the battalion history states, if so, it was not much good delaying things for only twenty-four hours.

Hook Trench lay 200 yards from the forward most British position in Hill Trench. In preparation for the postponed attack, white tape had been laid down in no man's land, thereby shortening the distance to the enemy trenches. This was an effective way of reducing casualties, especially during a night assault, yet the tape was left out between the lines during the day of 30 May, with fatal consequences for the assault. At 4p.m. on 30 May, Lieutenant-Colonel Campbell attended a conference at 86 Brigade HQ, where he received the final instructions for the attack: 86 Brigade were to capture Hook Trench from the 'block' at the junction with Tool Trench to point O.2.b.4.0 (about 800 yards due north).

The 86th Brigade were under the command of Brigadier-General Relf and the dispositions of the brigade at zero, 11.30p.m. on the 30th were as follows:

Right   8th East Lancashire Regiment. (37th Division)
Centre   1st Lancashire Fusiliers.
Left   16th Middlesex.[27]

The East Lancashire was to remove the 'block' in Tool Trench, for which they had formed a special 'unblocking party'. The remainder were to occupy that part of Hook Trench adjacent to the 'block' itself. If all went well those Germans in Tool Trench were to be pinched out from two sides. 'B' and 'D' Companies were to take up positions previously taped, with 'A' and 'C' in trenches further back. Coincidentally, at 11.20p.m., the Germans opened up a barrage on the front line and support

British troops watching shellfire close to Monchy-le-Preux.

trenches, though whether as a result of the capture of prisoners is not clear. More likely it was by chance, for a map found on a German officer indicated that a well-organised raid had been prepared against 29th Division that night. This may also have accounted for the marked vigilance and the degree of opposition that the troops were to encounter.[28] Whatever the cause, the artillery and machine-gun barrage fell on those men lying in the hastily scraped and taped line in no man's land.

Under the orders of the division, the forming-up line in no man's land was marked a by a white tape put down some forty-eight hours before the commencement of the attack. The natural result was that the enemy discovered the tape and arranged their counter-barrage accordingly.[29]

During the afternoon of 30 May, a very heavy thunderstorm struck the battlefield, causing the trenches to fill with water, when they had been relatively dry. The water caused Lewis guns and even rifles to jam and made movement very difficult.

At 11.30p.m. the British bombardment of Hook Trench by the artillery of six divisions began. Four minutes later, the barrage crept forward 100 yards and then a further 100 yards two minutes later. The salvoes crashed out for a further hour, trying to protect the advance, along with continuous bursts from twenty machine guns. The battalion advanced, all four companies quickly overrunning Hook Trench, in spite of very heavy machine-gun fire from shell holes further east. A German regimental history described these positions:

> The Ground that we had got to know two months ago still bore the imprint of the huge artillery battles that had taken place here. Whole areas were no more than rows of shell holes, the villages mere heaps of ruins. Bois du Vert, which lay just behind our lines, was a mound with tree stumps and huge craters. It looked like a gigantic sponge. To the north-west lay the ruins of Monchy. You could not speak of a position here: the forward positions lay out in the shell holes which formed the line as it had last been held.[30]

The East Lancashire bombers overtook the 'block' in Tool Trench and fought their way into Hook Trench. This was not without a cost. Corporal William Butterworth and Lance-Corporal Willie Denwood were part of the same bombing party that night.

Butterworth was reported to be 'wounded and missing' by a comrade who was detailed with a sergeant and seven others to:

Corporal William Butterworth. Image courtesy of the Denis Otter Collection.

Lance-Corporal Willie Denwood. Image courtesy of the Denis Otter Collection.

bomb the enemy trenches during a surprise attack on the Arras front. During the attack Corporal Butterworth was seen to fall, and when the muster was called, he and three others were found to be missing, including Private Denwood.[31]

Butterworth and Denwood were two men who typified the variety of different backgrounds found within the battalion. Their bodies were never recovered, their names remembered on the Arras Memorial.

William Butterworth was a twenty-five-year-old professional piano teacher from Burnley. His obituary in the *Burnley News* outlined his career:

He commenced his musical career when only twelve years of age, under the tutorship of Mr Jas. Armistead Mus. Bac. (Oxon) of Reedley. He obtained his elementary certificate for pianoforte playing under the Associated Board of the Royal Academy of Music and Royal College of Music in 1908, and passed the Intermediate Grade in 1909. In 1910 he succeeded in obtaining the advanced certificate.

His musical studies were fittingly rewarded in 1912, when he was awarded the 'Teachers' Certificate' by the Trinity College of Music, London, thereby admitting him to the position of Associate, and entitling him to use the letters A.T.C.L. It was about this time that he commenced as a professional teacher of the pianoforte. His thorough grasp of art, tactful bearing and kindly disposition, stood him in good stead and he was soon quoted as a most successful tutor, with a large number of pupils. He continued his profession to the time of enlistment in May, 1916.[32]

Lance-Corporal Denwood, by contrast, was a loom oiler in Burnley, though his home was at Cliviger in the rural parish outside the town. His father told the local paper that his son

Captain Walter Johnson Forster.
Image courtesy of the Steve Bury
Collection, Fulwood Barracks.

walked to work in Burnley in all weathers and was a good lad to his mother and home.
A keen footballer, Denwood played with the Mill Walk team, with whom he won many medals.
Married with three children, the twenty-nine year old advanced with the bombing party and
never returned:

> Of the nine men who went out, including an officer, four returned, the others were killed,
> Denwood having been found lying by the side of his officer, with whom he was a favourite.[33]

In the centre of Hook Trench troops had gained a strong foothold, though on the flanks the
position was more precarious. At 1.10a.m. the 8th Battalion war diary reported:

> Lieutenant Bentley O.C. 'D' Coy. reports in person that he got in the enemy trench
> with body of his men, but was unable to hold as his flanks were unprotected and had
> accordingly withdrawn to our front line. Enemy in large numbers had counter attacked
> from shell holes and had inflicted heavy casualties on us. Commanding Officer orders
> Lieutenant Bentley to gather as many men as he can from 'C' and 'D' Coys and with 'A'
> Coy reattack. (sic)[34]

During this time Captain Forster, commanding 'C' Company, was killed. Born in 1893 in
Nottingham, though a resident of Tunbridge Wells, Walter Johnson Forster was educated at
Trinity College, Oxford. He had from an early age shown keen interest in military matters,
serving for ten years with his school's Cadet Corps and then Oxford University Officers'
Training Corps. He was reading Law when war broke out, enlisted immediately and was
gazetted to the Special Reserve of the East Lancashire Regiment. He was posted to 1st East
Lancs and went to France in January 1915, being wounded the following March – losing the

CSM James Fleming.

thumb and first two fingers of his right hand – among other injuries. After a period of home training, he applied once more for active service, in spite of wounds that could have kept him at home. He was gazetted Captain and joined the 8th East Lancs in December 1916. Three accounts of his death gave an indication of the position in Hook Trench about 1a.m. Lieutenant-Colonel Campbell wrote to Forster's parents:

> We had been ordered to carry out a night attack, and Captain Forster reached the German Trenches with his men. The attack had only been partially successful, and his position was neither clear nor comfortable, and he had organised a defence, and then went along to find troops on his flank. A bullet struck him and he fell dead … It will doubtless be a source of pride to you to know that twice within ten days of his death he was congratulated by the Divisional General on his patrol work in a very difficult portion of the line.

A more informative account was told by Forster's second-in-command:

> I saw Captain Forster immediately our objective was gained, and he was then holding a German rifle and was quite merry and bright – in fact, joking over the ease with which we had accomplished it. Some time elapsed during which we were consolidating. Our covering parties then warned us that the enemy were advancing, and Lewis gun and rifle fire were opened out, with the result, as far as we were concerned, that this counter attack was beaten off. However, for some time we were bombed heavily from the front and suffered many casualties … The enemy succeeded eventually in entering the trench on both flanks and were gradually working up to us in large parties, bombing every yard as they came. No sooner did the men pass down the news that they were in the trench on the right than Captain Forster and his servant went to the scene of the action and endeavoured to hold up this movement by

throwing bombs. At the same time I was engaged on the left on the same job, and only heard later that Captain Forster had been hit.

One of the other ranks described Forster's death:

> Captain Forster was hit in the stomach, and died at once. I was in the same bay at the time and saw him hit. He only spoke four words – asked for a drink of water – and died. The two officers were wonderful. They were not only up and down the trench, keeping the men in good heart, but they did excellent work with the bombs themselves. The part they played has been the talk of the battalion since.[35]

Forster's name is inscribed on the Arras Memorial.

By 2.20a.m., all the companies had withdrawn and orders were received from 86 Brigade that there was to be no further counter-attack and that the battalion should 'stand fast' on its original line. During the withdrawal, there were many acts of heroism, none more so than the actions of CSM Fleming of 'D' Company. Aged twenty-nine and employed at Chanter's Pit in Atherton, Fleming had originally enlisted in the Manchester Regiment in early October 1914, before being immediately transferred to the East Lancashires. Rapid promotion followed, arrested only by wounds suffered at Hannescamps in June 1916 (*see* chapter two). Fleming was treated in Aberdeen, before returning to the battalion in the early part of 1917. The citation to the award of the Distinguished Conduct Medal during the action of the early morning of 31 May reads as follows:

> For conspicuous gallantry and devotion to duty during an attack upon the enemy trenches. He led his company with great courage, and when finally a withdrawal was ordered he remained till the last to see that it was properly carried out. He was three times wounded.

Following further recuperation in a Liverpool hospital, Fleming, a devout Catholic, returned to to his native Hindsford, where he was presented with his DCM at Tyldesley Catholic Club. He also received a marble clock and two elegant bronze statues in recognition of his conduct. He was to join the 11th Battalion in 1918 as a Warrant Officer* and, in June of that year, won a Military Cross, which was later presented to him by the King at Buckingham Palace. In 1938 James Fleming served overseas once more, after offering his services to the Royal British Legion, to help to oversee the arrangements for a plebiscite in Czechoslovakia, part of the Munich Agreement of 1938. He served again during 1939–45 and lived until 1967. A man of faith, duty and courage, Fleming always carried with him a small leather pouch that contained a miniature page from the Bible to give him strength during difficult times.

The attack on Hook Trench resulted in the deaths of three officers, and seventy other men becoming casualties. The battalion was bussed to the west of Arras for further training. There was to be no return to the Arras battlefields until after the war, when the 37th Division Memorial was unveiled at the heart of Monchy-le-Preux village.

The battalion didn't yet know it, but the days left to the 8th East Lancs were numbered. Its soldiers would be involved in one further campaign – what became known as the 3rd Battle for Ypres and more popularly as the battle for Passchendaele.

THE PASSCHENDAELE CAMPAIGN – 1917

2nd Lieutenant Milton Riley

Among the officers and other ranks drafted into the battalion in the early part of June 1917 was 2nd Lieutenant Milton Riley from Blackburn. Born in 1898, Riley was only nineteen years old when he joined the 8th East Lancs on 11 June at Dennebroeucq, a small French village, thirteen miles south-west of St Omer. Educated at King Edward VII School at Lytham in Lancashire, Riley had been a senior prefect and captain of the rugby 1st XV. Eldest brother Herbert had joined the Army at the outbreak of war, while another sibling Harold had followed into the East Lancashire Territorials six months later. Having passed the entrance exam for Sandhurst, Riley promptly failed the medical examination and was forced to pursue other routes into officer training. He successfully made the grade with The Inns of Court Officer Training Corps and was posted to 3rd East Lancs at Plymouth in April 1917, completing his instruction in the Bull Ring* at Etaples two months later.

Milton Riley left two narratives of his time in the 8th East Lancashires, from June 1917 until the battalion was disbanded early in 1918. One undated script is handwritten and was perhaps penned soon after the war, the other completed in 1970 after a lifetime's reflection. Both texts provide insights into the operation of the 8th East Lancs during the battles around the Ypres salient, as well as sketching out the parts played by men of all ranks.

> It was a nice evening when we arrived. The band was giving a concert. Major Courtney, the second-in-command gave us dinner at the headquarters mess … We found Cunliffe (commanding 'A' Company, *see* Chapter 5) very good natured and a good leader, who could be firm in a modest way. He had been through very stiff fighting in the Gavrelle area and won the Military Cross as a result …
>
> The Commanding Officer, Lieutenant-Colonel Hon. Ian M Campbell, invited the new officers to dinner at Headquarters during the short stay at Dennebroeucq, regaling us on strawberries, gathered I believe, in the garden of the small chateau. I consider myself fortunate in joining his battalion. He was most courteous and considerate to us all. The battalion ran itself very smoothly under his command.[1]

Battalion training at Dennebroeucq lasted a fortnight, much attention being paid to musketry and what was termed 'open warfare' – preparation for any forthcoming breakthrough in the trench stalemate. Night exercises were again practised, as was the continued development of the weapon specialists. However, the battalion history was at pains to point out that:

2nd Lieutenant Milton Riley. Image
courtesy of Fulwood Barracks.

The training programme laid down by division was, in the opinion of many, far too strenuous, no time at all being allowed for recreation or games and everyone was pleased when on the 22nd June we started north by road, reaching the Locre area on June 25th.[2]

No one should have been surprised for, as the battalion was inspected, Milton Riley was reminded of the divisional general's reputation:

The next day we marched past our two generals – Brigadier-General R.C. Maclachlan, GOC of 112 Brigade and Major-General H. Bruce-Williams, GOC 37th Division, who was known affectionately as 'Bloody Bill'. Each new arrival to his division received a leaflet – 'Yes, we'll do it. What is it?'

Indeed, the battalion's movement up to Locre was marked by three days of intensive marching ordered by division, which resulted in sixty-five men falling out of the line of march as they approached their destination after crossing the Franco-Belgian frontier. Many of the new conscripts had to be helped along the way, as Riley remembered:

Brigadier Maclachlan, smiled approvingly on a perspiring subaltern carrying two rifles, as well as a pack. Some of the men were wanting to fall out with bad feet or bad heart and I helped the weary ones.

That was not the end of the matter, for the following day 'Bloody Bill' personally inspected those men who had fallen out during the march up to the Ypres salient. The battalion was being hardened for the task ahead.

Locre, and its neighbour Dranoutre, are small Belgian settlements, several of which sit at the heart of the Flanders Hills: Kemmel, Mont des Cats, Mont Noir, Mont Rouge and The

Men taking part in a church service.

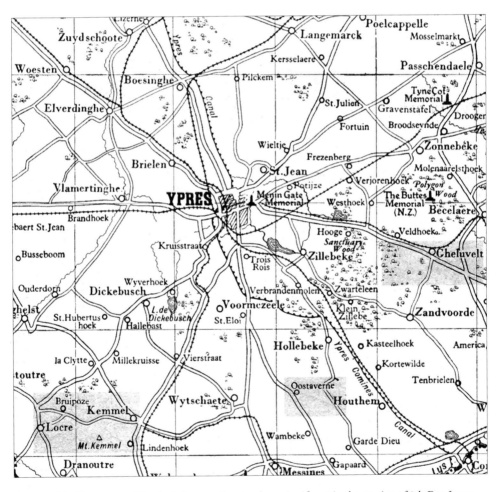

A map of the Ypres sector. The shaded areas relate to places significant in the service of 8th East Lancs during their time in and around the salient.

Scherpenberg. Lying between the two villages, and approximately seven miles south-west of Ypres, the 8th East Lancs made their way to Wakefield Huts. This camp was situated in a wooded valley in the shadow of Mont Rouge and was one of the sites to which the battalion would return for much of July. The first few days saw a lessening of intensive training, with time given over to recreational activities – a cricket match against the 7th Battalion, which was billeted nearby, a revolver competition and a boxing tournament. Baths were made available once a week, and on Sunday 8 July there was a Church Parade for the whole battalion.

Attendance on Church Parade on Sunday was mandatory, regardless of whether men were Methodists, Baptists, Catholics or Anglicans. Out on rest, drum-head services were the norm, with men paraded in such a way as to form three sides of a square (atheists were not exempt but were allowed to turn their backs on proceedings). To many soldiers, such services were nothing more than a duty, and they sang hymns, typically *Onward Christian Soldiers* and *Fight the good Fight*, for padres were kept on a short leash by the Army for fear that too many sermons about 'loving thine enemy' might soften Tommy's willingness to kill.[3]

Third Ypres: The Battle of Passchendaele – Background

By the summer of 1917, the British carried the main responsibility for continuing the offensive on the Western Front. The armies of France remained on the defensive after their losses and mutinies in April and May and American troops would not enter the war zone in any numbers until 1918. Looking back, the Commander-in-Chief, Sir Douglas Haig, outlined his purposes for the opening of a new battle in his despatch of 25 December 1917:

> The positions held by us in the Ypres salient since May 1915, were far from satisfactory. They were completely overlooked by the enemy. Their defence involved a considerable strain on the troops occupying them, and they were certain to be costly to maintain against a serious attack, in which the enemy would enjoy all the advantages in observation and in the placing of his artillery. Our positions would be much improved by the capture of the Messines-Wytschaete Ridge and of the high ground which extends thence north-eastwards for some seven miles and then trends north through Broodseinde and Passchendaele.[4]

There were other strategic reasons also. The attack in Flanders would draw German reserves away from positions opposite the war-weary French and, if successful, provide an opportunity to capture U-boat bases along the Belgian coast, at a time when Allied shipping losses were reaching critical levels. In addition, the new offensive would take the heat off the Russian Army faced with revolution and provide a chance to capture Roulers, one of the keys to the German strategic railway network.

Oostaverne

It was for these reasons that the 8th East Lancs had been summoned north, though throughout the campaign, the battalion would usually be involved in diversionary actions to the main fighting. Formally entitled as 'The Battles of Ypres 1917', the campaign is popularly known as 'Passchendaele'. At first, 112 Brigade was involved in working parties behind the Oostaverne sector of the front. Though, as Milton Riley recalled, there was never a safe time in a war zone:

> It was on the way back from one of these night working parties that I saw first a serious casualty. As we were coming down the ridge, one of our own shells, owing to a faulty driving

Two 8th East Lancashire Officers, Lob and Smith, supervising a working party at Lucheux in 1916. Image courtesy of the Imperial War Museum, London. Ref. 06771. Also Mr Tom Yuille.

band, dropped some hundreds of yards away and one of the party of North Lancashires was badly hit in the stomach. By the light of the matches, he was attended to in a very bad way and looking ghastly. I vividly recollect the shock with which I first heard the sickening cry of 'stretcher-bearers!'

From the slopes of Kemmel Hill, Riley was also struck for the first time by the extent of the undertaking in which he was involved:

There was a panoramic view at night, of the various illuminations from the line. Gun flashes and rocketing signal lights and observation lights were accompanied by lively sounds, the dull rumbling of artillery and the staccato crackling of machine guns. The serious work of watching and waiting and hindering movements, and interrupting communications, with here a patrol and there a raid, was going on from the coast down to Arras, with an intensity full of significance. It was beginning to look to me a very war-like war.

Preparations for the front line were made in the middle of July. There were lectures on trench sanitation, gas equipment was tested and iron rations and underwear carefully checked and replaced where necessary. The men took baths in Kemmel, had their clothing disinfected and their feet checked by their platoon commanders. All weapons and ammunition were made ready.

The 37th Division was to hold that part of the front approximately five miles due south of the city of Ypres. The four-mile march via Kemmel and eastwards through Wychaete took the battalion to trenches close to a small hamlet called Oostarverne. 'The Third Ypres' offensive was to start on 31 July and it was from this sector, from jumping-off positions close to Oostaverne, that the men would once more go over the top. The area was east of the Messines ridge, successfully captured with the aid of nineteen mines exploded under the German lines earlier in June.

It had been rolling pasture, cut through with numerous small streams into which water drained from the lush fields. Woods and copses dominated the landscape at its northern end, though the defining feature was the large number of farms strewn out across the shallow valleys. Many of these farms had been made defensible by the Germans. Pillboxes dotted the German defensive line, the ground unsuitable for the construction of deep dugouts. When the 'Third Battle of Ypres' began, the sandy clays turned into a morass, as the drainage system collapsed in the face of shellfire and much higher than average rainfall.

Meanwhile, at Wychaete, 'A' Company officers met the guides of the battalion being relieved by the East Lancs. Second Lieutenant Riley, already anxious about his first tour of duty, found little comfort in the discussion:

> We met the 'Guides' somewhere near Wychaete, after passing through some of our artillery, which was rather noisy. As I was walking in front with Cunliffe I heard the conversation with the guides about the conditions 'in front'. As we quietly filed into a communication trench, one of them very gloomily informed us that we might as well be dead as alive, that the shelling in this sector was very intense and that their casualties had been numerous.

The battalion took over the front line beyond York Trench, with supports 200 yards further back. 'D' Company held a line of shell holes in advanced positions. To men in the line for the first time, the enemy artillery fire was an ordeal:

> The trench I was in, had at the sides, small cavities, which we called 'cubby holes'. I spent several hours in one of these when the Germans put down a heavy barrage along the sector from about three am 'til dawn of July 20th. In my report I rather stressed the bombardment as 'terrific'. It was nevertheless, rather terrifying for a novice. It was a bit like an earthquake to me and I felt very scared. But severe as these bombardments were, this was a very ordinary affair for The Salient in 1917.[5]

There was some respite from the shelling for the officers in a position previously occupied by the enemy:

> I rested at 'A' Company HQ, which was a concrete pill box some 200 yards to the rear. It was of the usual style, the entrance faced the Germans, and was shielded by an inner wall. A wall, at right angles to this, divided the squat structure into two rooms, each of which had a slit window space intended for a machine gun facing the British. One portion was used for the company runners, orderlies, cook signallers and Company Sergeant-Major. The other, supplied with wood and wire bunks, and a rough table and box seats, was the Office and Bedroom and Mess of the company Commander Cunliffe and the officers with him. The place was dimly lighted by candles, stuck in bottlenecks.[6]

Much to Riley's relief, the tour of the trenches ended on 26 July, when the Lancashires passed along the wooden duckboard road back to Wakefield Huts at Locre. A few days later, he was sent to the IX Corps School on a company Officers' Training Course, which would last for almost a month. He was to miss the opening attack of the 'Third Ypres' campaign on 31 July, no doubt a little relieved, writing:

> My first tour was completed. It did not seem to have bothered anybody else, but I had found it a bit of an ordeal, but just tolerable.

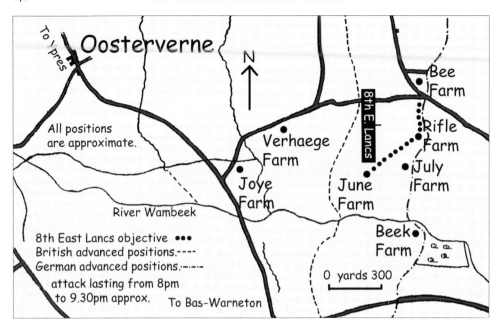

The attack by the 8th East Lancs on Rifle Farm during the first day of the Third Battle of Ypres, 31 July 1917.

The Battle of Pilckem Ridge – 31 July 1917

The first of the successive stages, of what came to be known as the 'Third Ypres', was the Battle of Pilckem Ridge. Pilckem was two miles north of Ypres, sitting astride the first strategically important high ground to be captured in the battle. The 37th Division was part of IX Corps, holding the trenches in front of Oostaverne, south of the salient. IX Corp's role was to pin those Germans opposite, preventing them from transferring to the front of the Fifth Army where the main attack was to take place. Meanwhile, 37th Division was to capture the advanced German line from the Blauweportebeek on the right to Rifle Farm on the left. The battalions of 112 Brigade were once more in reserve at zero hour – 3.50a.m. and the 8th East Lancs were only sent forward to support 4th Middlesex at midday.

Since early morning, the rain had poured and the ground was beginning to take the muddy form which has become forever synonymous with the Ypres salient. The battalion moved forward towards the advanced line, in search of the three companies of 4th Middlesex, from whom their GOC had heard nothing. Throughout the afternoon, the men were in support of the continuing attacks, awaiting orders to go forward. After several false alarms, 'A', 'B' and 'C' Companies were ordered to attack at 8p.m. A curtain barrage was maintained 150 yards beyond the objectives and the battalion advanced on a platoon frontage in three waves – 'C' on the left towards Bee Farm, 'A' in the centre to Rifle Farm and 'B' on the right in the direction of July Farm. Rifle Farm had concealed a pillbox among the buildings, but the latter had been demolished by artillery, leaving only the sinister ferro-concrete structure standing.

The ground rose gently from the jumping-off positions. Initially, all went well, all companies reporting that they had achieved their objectives, had driven back the opposition at the point of a bayonet and were digging in. Yet the flanks of their position were in the air, despite efforts to send out patrols to find the neighbouring units. The Germans heavily barraged their positions, which, along with the fact that the weapons were choked with mud and new enemy

Strohgut bei Zonnebeke. Haus dient zur Maskierung eines Beton-
unterftandes (rechts)   Gefr. Lorenz

A farmhouse typical of the salient, enclosing a German pillbox. Image courtesy of Malte Znaniecki.

reinforcements had appeared, forced the battalion to retire. It was after midnight. The battalion had attacked once more with great courage, but with little luck. Eighteen men had been killed, seventy-three were wounded and eleven were missing.

Private William Turner, from Burnley, a member of the National Reserve and one of the few surviving members of the battalion to embark in France, was killed in the attack. The thirty-three year old was a collector with the local Weavers' Association at Woodfield Mill. Married with one son, Turner had received no wound of any kind until his death, some of the time having been spent as an officer's servant. The officer had given to him a pocket watch, pipe and cigarette case in appreciation of his services and these mementoes had been passed on to his son. William Turner's body was not recovered and his name is remembered on the Menin Gate Memorial at Ypres.[7] Another casualty of the attack was Lance-Sergeant James Tomlinson. A friend of Tomlinson's stated that:

> He was leading his men when he was shot through the arm. He went on for a considerable distance and then dropped. He was very well respected by his men and his loss will be deeply deplored.[8]

Captain Cunliffe wrote to Tomlinson's sister, telling her that although he wasn't present at the time, he had established that her brother had been hit in the spine by a sniper. Cunliffe regarded Tomlinson highly, especially as an instructor and someone who got on with his job 'without grousing'. His sweetheart Elsie wrote the following in the local paper not long after his death:

> Some may think that I forget him
> When at times they see me smile,
> But they little know the sorrow
> That smile's hiding all the while.

Private William Turner. Image courtesy of the
Denis Otter Collection.

Lance-Sergeant James Tomlinson. Image courtesy
of the Rossendale Free Press.

> Only those who have loved and lost
>   Know the meaning of the word 'Gone'.

Twenty-one years old, Tomlinson had enlisted in April 1915, leaving his bleaching job at Holme
Mill, in his native Rawtenstall. He, too, is remembered on the Menin Gate Memorial.

By the end of the day, conditions were appalling, as Guy Chapman remembered:

> The battle opened in mist and rumour. The rumours proved false, and the mist turned to
> drizzle, to rain and then to a savage torrent, in which the sky competed with the guns, and
> conquered. The sullen gun fire died away. Le bon dieu Bosche had won again. The battlefield
> was said to be flooded. Wounded were drowning in shell holes. All fighting had ceased, while
> the infantry sat miserably casting one preference against another, death by water or by fire. On
> the next morning, the trickling brook behind our huts had risen three feet and quadrupled its
> width, and its brown flood was reflected in the upper air.[9]

Officers and Gentlemen

Just before dawn on 1 August, parties of men went out to search for the wounded, and all that
were brought in were sent successfully down the line for treatment. There was no time to
recover the dead. That evening the battalion was relieved and went back to Wakefield Huts at
Locre. Two days later a congratulatory message was received by Lieutenant-Colonel Campbell
from Brigadier-General Maclachlan, GOC 112 Brigade:

> I wish to put on record my appreciation of the conduct of the battalion under your command
> on the evening of 31st July. I hear that the advance to Rifle Farm was first rate and fully up to

MAJOR-GEN. H. BRUCE WILLIAMS, C.B., D.S.O.,
G.-O.-C. 37th DIVISION
Drawn by Interpreter P. F. Robinet

Brigadier-General R.C. Maclachlan, GOC of 112 Brigade until he was killed by a sniper on 11 August 1917.

Major-General H. Bruce-Williams, GOC of 37th Division from October 1916 to the Armistice.

the old traditions of the regiment. I am convinced that the position was gallantly gained, and could, and would have been held if the weather conditions had been different.

However, I understand that no rifle or Lewis gun could be kept in action owing to mud, and, therefore, the advanced position became too dangerous to hold.

It is hard luck that all the good work should have been spoiled by an unlucky change.[10]

It was to be one of the last missives from Maclachlan. He was killed by a sniper on 11 August, having been revered by the battalion's officers, as one who was based at Brigade HQ recounted at the time of the Brigadier's death:

In the battalion we had come to regard General Maclachlan with an affection not often extended to the Staff. He knew every subaltern and never met any of us without a kindly greeting. His manner towards us was perfectly easy, and we, in our turn felt able to talk to him in a natural manner and with none of that defensive attitude of mind which the sight of a brass hat instinctively evoked. It was only when I got to Brigade Headquarters that I realised how practical and deep an interest he took in the comfort and well being of his brigade. Any little scheme for easing the burden of the troops was sure of his instant and whole-hearted support, and he would immediately set the necessary arrangements in motion. In these matters he was ably seconded by Captain Lewis, the brigade major. When the brigade was in the line he would say, 'Come along Lewis, let's see how the Bedfords (or whatever the battalion might be) are getting on; they've got a rotten section of the line.' And the two would don Mackintoshes and sally out to see what could be done to help. Another favourite companion was Colonel Dill, the GSO1 of the division, and it was with Colonel Dill that the General was making his rounds when he was killed. I well remember how much everyone at Brigade Headquarters was affected when the news arrived. One man simply buried his head in his hands and wept, and when, a little later, I was helping the Staff

Captain Robert Wilson Cunliffe.
Image courtesy of Peter Cunliffe.

Captain to pack up the General's effects for dispatch to England, we both felt like doing the same.[11]

Though it was understandable that a more distant relationship should exist between a battalion and its Divisional General, Major-General Bruce-Williams was a different individual altogether, as another officer attached temporarily to 'Bloody Bill's Staff witnessed:

> An atmosphere of uneasiness and irritability hung over our headquarters. General Bruce-Williams believed in keeping his staff up to the mark and the two senior staff officers carried out his creed with Calvinistic thoroughness. The result was Genevan; absolute efficiency and complete unhappiness. Junior officers wore the faces of the hunted, as they crept out of the offices and fled with furtive hurrying steps from the building, gloomily shaking the fleas from their ears. The entrance of the burly figure of our general caused a minor stampede among the learners in Q office. In G there was a comparative calm. The placidity of the GSO 2 and 3 frequently averted the whip; and so long as we were busy being busy, we could rely on our obscurity for shelter, when the thunder roared.[12]

New junior officers could also have an uneasy relationship with experienced NCOs, on whom the former inevitably relied for guidance, particularly when first in the trenches. Milton Riley characterised 'A's Company Sergeant-Major as a 'sadistic specimen'. During his first trench tour he described the following encounter:

> I stood on the fire-step appalled and probably wide eyed, with the inferno of an attack so near. Nearby was the sardonic CSM. In the presence of men of my platoon he said, with a nasty grin, 'When we go over on the 31st, I'm going next to you Sir.' Somewhat coldly I replied 'Why, Sergeant-Major?' Then came the punch line – 'Because Sir,' he said, 'I like your wrist watch!'

An 8th East Lancs working party quarrying at Henu in 1916. Steel helmets were only issued from the spring of 1916 onwards, some of the men here adopting the knotted handkerchief option while behind the lines! Image courtesy of the Imperial War Museum, London. Ref. 0677/1. Also Mr Tom Yuille.

Riley was fortunate in having a confident and experienced senior officer such as Captain Cunliffe as his immediate superior. Cunliffe took a paternal approach with inexperienced subalterns and supported them in a variety of ways – sending them on courses when they were in need of rest, ensuring that the workload was evenly spread among them and when confronted with difficult NCOs. Sergeant Baker, who had won the DCM at Arras (*see* Chapter 5), was apt to be truculent:

> Baker I think had little time for most of us. When I was still new to the battalion I was given the job of paying out the company. Sat beside me was a Warrant Officer with a pay sheet, on which the amount to be paid to each one was shown. This amount depended not only on rank, but on how much a man was in credit. I had the money, in notes of five francs upwards, and as each man came to the table and saluted his name was quietly called out and the amount I had to give him. And, at the time, I was the only subaltern in 'A' Company.
>
> Sergeant Baker, no doubt on his binges, had spent too much to have any money left. But as a special favour he was to receive a token payment of five francs, say in our money 3*s* 6*d*. As he put out his hand to take his pay, I gave him the huge sum allowed. Looking rather disgusted, Baker kept his hand out holding the five francs and said to me – 'This is no good to me Sir!' But Captain Cunliffe just then arrived and came to the table from behind me, and answered Baker for me, saying 'Very well, Baker give it back to Mr Riley.' Which of course he did, saluted and marched off.[13]

Riley had a better relationship with another DCM winner, Sergeant Wells:

> with whom I used to sit in the line and play football behind it, when we tried our best to charge one another, by fair charge, into a shell-hole, as part of the fun.

As Riley's confidence and experience grew, so Captain Cunliffe came to rely on him more, as Cunliffe himself became wearier and his nerve diminished:

> I resumed my meal, but only a few minutes later, Cunliffe and Reynolds returned, white faced and momentarily silent. Then Cunliffe said 'A sniper got Jarintzoff. (one of the other company COs.) Will you go and get his personal belongings out of his pockets to send home? We just couldn't.' In the trench, some forty or so yards from the pillbox was Jarintzoff's body. The back of his skull was quite blown out by a bullet that must have had the nose filed, a dum-dum bullet. I was told later that his mother, a widow, was a keen spiritualist.

Interlude

After a period of rest and re-equipping, 8th East Lancs and the 37th Division 'side stepped' one divisional place north, taking over on the Ypres side of Oostaverne. The battalion went into the line once more on 11 August, and it was during a tour of the front line the following day that Maclachlan was killed. Four days later, an East Lancs patrol was visiting one of their advanced posts in no man's land and discovered that the position was empty. No sounds had been heard, nor warnings given. Two unexploded German grenades pointed to the snatching of Corporal Hargreaves and four other ranks by a German patrol and taken prisoner.

On 26 August, 2nd Lieutenant Riley returned to the battalion from training. From the time of his arrival the rain fell consistently heavily. The trenches filled with water, baling out a constant necessity. No man's land had turned into a lake, deterring both sides from serious action, even the recently installed 'storm troops' opposite. The East Lancs were relieved two days later by 13th Rifle Brigade, a pitiful event as Riley recalled:

> The incoming troops, many of them very young, were late. The journey over mud, well sprinkled with shell holes almost full of water, had been very unpleasant. Some of the men

A draft of conscripts destined for France during 1917. Image courtesy of Fulwood Barracks.

had been stuck fast, with the result that, in being hauled out, they had left their waterproof gumboots in the mud, and in some cases were in their socks, having slung their boots over their equipment. They were very distressed and some of them were weeping.[14]

The first three weeks of September 1917 were spent for the most part in working parties, moving up supplies to the front line. The majority involved carrying materials used to maintain trench structures, or enable better movement in the appalling conditions. Milton Riley kept a 'chit' for one such journey:

> To Officer i/c of Carrying Party.
> Please carry to IMPERIAL AVENUE
> 150 'A' Frames.*
> 110 sheets of c.i. (corrugated iron)
> 50 Trench Boards.
> This ought to take six journeys, taking about 3 & a half hours.
>
> T.G. Caddick-Adams.
> O.C. 'A' Coy.
> 9th North Staffs.

I remember that journey well. There was a fair amount of shelling and we reduced the number of journeys by carrying double loads. It was not very rapid progress, as a rule, with men carrying long sheets of corrugated iron, over duckboard tracks, and sometimes down narrow communication trenches.

Hill 60

With a fighting strength of only 300, and at two hours' notice, the East Lancashires were ordered up into the trenches closer to Ypres itself on 22 September. They paraded at 5p.m. and took buses from their camp towards the city. The 37th Division had been ordered into the line, in position just south of the Menin Road, opposite Gheluvelt. The 112 Brigade, including the battalion, was in reserve in the Hill 60 area. However, they were needed almost immediately to go into the trenches in front of the Hill itself while an attack was in progress.

The 'Hill' was formed by the spoil taken from the cutting through which the railway ran and got its name because the resultant feature is 60 metres above sea level. Much of the fighting here had been underground, from the moment that the French had lost the hill to the Germans in 1914, to the British gaining control of it again in April 1915, only to lose it again the following year. It had finally come back into British hands, when captured as part of the attack at Messines. In the flat landscape around Ypres, possession of the hill was thought vital by both sides. The area was pitted with mine craters and shell holes and many of those who had dug the tunnels and worked the black clay corridors are still entombed there.

The men made their way in the dark up to the front, their officers relatively unprepared in this part of the line and it was quite by chance that Milton Riley, leading 'A' Company up to the front, missed a turning and halted his men. 'B' Company followed the correct route though, at a certain point, they too had to halt when a 5.9" shell landed among one of the platoons, killing over twenty men. It was the single biggest loss of its type of the war. Among the dead were Privates Warth, Dent and Robinson.

Second Lieutenant Speak wrote to the wife of Private Arthur Warth from Burnley:

Private Arthur Warth. Image courtesy
of the Denis Otter Collection.

> We were going in the trenches when two shells dropped right among us, killing your husband
> and a number of comrades. His death was instantaneous.

Thirty-two years old, Warth was one of the latest recruits, having enlisted in January 1917.
Described as having a quiet disposition, Warth had been a laundry worker before joining up
and was closely connected with the Ebenezer church, where he had been elected an elder. He
had been an organist there for many years, as well as the teacher of the young men's class. Yet it
was his involvement in putting on children's entertainments organised by the church that he
was best remembered. He has no known grave and is remembered on the Tyne Cot Memorial
at Zonnebeke.[15]

The first that Mr and Mrs Dent heard of the death of their son, Private Herbert Dent, was
from an Army chaplain, to the effect that he had died on 23 September from wounds sustained
the previous day. A few days later, an official communication was received by them, saying only
that Herbert had been wounded on 22 September. Their anxiety was heightened in the same
postal delivery, by a letter from one of Herbert's comrade's – Private W.H. Bromley:

Dear Mr & Mrs Dent,

   No doubt you will be surprised to hear from me, but I feel I ought to write to you about
your son, Herbert. He was standing in the trenches on Sunday 23rd, when an enemy shell
burst nearby, wounding him very severely in the legs. Fortunately, there was an aid post a few
yards away, where he received immediate attention. I went to the dressing station as soon as
I heard about him, but unfortunately, I was not allowed to see him, because they were very
busy at the time. I was very sorry, as I was certain I could have cheered him up if nothing else.
I have not heard anything of his condition, but I sincerely trust that he will make a speedy
recovery. I can assure you I miss him greatly, because we attended the same day school, and

Private Herbert Dent. Image courtesy of the
Denis Otter Collection.

Private Harry Robinson. Image courtesy of the
Denis Otter Collection.

further had many things in common which gave rise to interesting discussion. I am enclosing
a book of music that came out of his pack. It will be a great trouble to you, but I hope that
you will be able to bear the sad news with a brave heart, which will undoubtedly help him to
make a speedy recovery.[16]

The Army chaplain had been with Dent when he had died; having lost one leg and being
severely wounded in the other and was buried at La Clytte Military Cemetery. The return of
the book of music reflected everything that had been important in the life of Herbert Dent.
Although employed in the cotton industry, he was well known in Burnley as a talented pianist
and teacher of music. He was reputed to be exceptionally talented on the pianoforte, winning
an open competition prior to the outbreak of war. In a letter home, just prior to his death,
Dent had asked about the condition of his beloved piano, and the sheet music removed from
his pack was an album of his beloved Chopin's waltzes that he had acquired in France.[17]

Private Harry Robinson also died of his wound on 23 September. Robinson had been a
travelling salesman by trade, but it was as a celebrated elocutionist that he was best known
in the Padiham area, where reputedly his skills were much in demand. He performed
Shakespeare – his last performance was *As You Like It* with the Burnley Amateurs – and
gave much of his time over to charity work, a product of his upbringing with the Padiham
Unitary Sunday School. He had learned his acting and oration skills as a boy through the
school's connection to the Old Dramatic Society. Thirty-eight years old, Harry Robinson
left a widow and four children. He is buried at Outtersteene Communal Military Cemetery
Extension at Bailleul.[18]

The Battles of Broodseinde – 4 October 1917 – and Poelcappelle – 9 October 1917

During the night of the 27 to 28 September, the 37th Division went into the line in the Ypres salient proper. The previous day, 39th Division had gained a foothold on the strategically important Tower Hamlets ridge, which ran at right angles south of the Menin Road, opposite to Gheluvelt. The 37th Division relieved the 39th, holding the trench line on the eastern slopes of Tower Hamlets ridge closest to the road, yet as the trenches wound south they crossed the crest until in the southern sector they ran onto the western slopes.

At this time in the campaign, the division's role was once more to simulate attacks along their front, pinning the German's reserves behind Gheluvelt. These feints and simulated actions would be in support of two major offensives in the salient north of the Menin Road – Broodseinde and Poelcappelle. During late September, the British High Command believed that German morale and reserves were diminishing as a result of the 'bite and hold'* tactics championed by General Plumer. More assaults were needed to maintain the momentum. The rain held off during the end of September, only to return early in October.

The extreme conditions experienced by the 8th East Lancs during their forthcoming tour of the trenches, from 4–11 October, were arguably the worst the battalion had ever faced. One or two men remembered bad conditions at Foncquevillers in the winter of 1915, some the atrocious ground on the Redan Ridge in 1916, while others recalled the snow and filth opposite Monchy-le-Preux the previous April. Yet, in terms of the state of the ground; the difficulties of resupply and reinforcement; the dangers and weather conditions faced and the length of the tour, this period would be the harshest yet.

Having spent some of the period at the end of September in tunnels under Hill 60, the 8th East Lancashire were involved in the usual carrying and working parties behind the line. On 4 October the companies were moved forward, attached to other 37th Division units that were making a feint attack, attempting to draw fire from artillery batteries beyond Gheluvelt. To reach the front line men had to pass along makeshift duckboard roads, which were often pinpointed by the enemy's artillery. Men who slipped off the boards often drowned in the mire on either side, the wounded having little chance of survival and the dead left unburied. Shell holes were filled with putrid water, corpses and the detritus of war. This swathe of mud reached as far as the eye could see, broken only by the shattered stumps of trees and the outlines of pillboxes – the essential Passchendaele landscape.

From his position in the reserve line in what was left of Bodmin Copse, 2nd Lieutenant Milton Riley, with 'A' and 'B' Companies, was to make his way his way forward over the morass

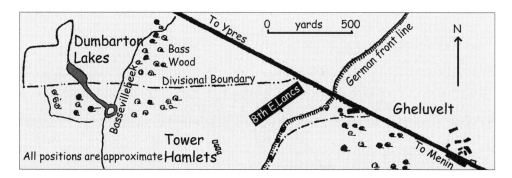

The battalion's position in the line opposite Gheluvelt from 6–11 October 1917. Some soldiers thought this period their worst in the line during the war.

A duckboard walkway across the mire. An easy target for artillery, men could drown by losing their way. Falling off the walkway when wounded often proved fatal.

that was the Bassevillebeek, cross the marshy ground of Dumbarton Lakes and go into the support trenches between the captured German defensive positions of Tower Hamlets and the Menin Road. The Tower Hamlets ridge protected the men from direct observation, but the Germans, who had until recently occupied the positions on the ridge, continuously plastered the area of the Bassevillebeek with high explosives. Riley's CO, Captain Cunliffe, had delayed moving forward initially from the copse, for the shelling was severe. So severe in fact that men became hysterical, some having to be held down, such was the ferocity of the bombardment. Eventually, during the early afternoon of 4 October, the bombardment died down sufficiently for a rum ration to be issued. Finally, led by guides from another battalion, the men made their way forward.

> We went slowly, and, after a time stopped. The guides were lost! They said they had been using some ruined tanks as a land mark, but they had proved to be the wrong ones. They asked us to wait while they searched for the duckboard track we should be on … After some twenty minutes the guides found us and told us the glad news that they had found the direction. We moved on, and came to the duckboard track, which was the only path across a very swampy barrier called the Bassevillebeek. At the other side was a ridge – Tower Hamlets. Beyond the crest was the Support Trench we had to reach. The Germans had very recently been in possession of the large 'pillbox' at Tower Hamlets and knew all about the path leading to it. Probably, they had guns firing on it, in relays, day and night. Just as we got on the track – ROAR! A 'strafe' was on. Shells, showers of them, crashed and 'crumped' and roared and 'plopped' all around us. It was deafening and the air was pungent with picric acid, and our heads 'buzzed' and 'sang' with the din, and concussion. But for the mud we should never have come through it.[19]

Riley and the rest of 'A' and 'B' Companies reached the support trenches, which were not revetted, and were deep and narrow. In the early hours of 5 October these companies took over

German prisoners, a working party and stretcher-bearers photographed together during the Battle of Broodseinde, 4 October 1917.

the front line opposite Gheluvelt. During that first day they were heavily shelled, with six of Riley's men being killed, including a soldier from Blackburn called Private John Kelly.

He was described by Riley as 'a patient quiet lad of eighteen, who came from Blackburn, my native town, and I sent a letter of sympathy to his mother a widow. He was her only son.' In the letter Riley mentioned that he was from Blackburn and, the following year, having seen Riley's name in the local press, Mrs Kelly wrote to his parents to express her thanks and hoping for his safe return. Close bonds were common between a comrades of a dead soldier, the last to see him alive, and families in mourning. Nineteen years old, Private John Kelly had worked at the Star Paper Mill prior to enlisting at the age of sixteen. He was retained in England and then served for fourteen months in France prior to his death. An officer, probably Riley himself, wrote to his mother:

> Your laddie was always an example to the younger and stronger men. Never was there a soldier more willing and dutiful. At all times he kept bright and cheery. For his cheeriness, especially in the face of bereavement he suffered some time ago (the death of his father) he was liked and respected by all. I deeply regret his loss.[20]

The letter also told Mrs Kelly only that her son had died instantly as a result of a shell burst. Riley described the event in greater detail, telling how a Lance-Corporal disobeyed orders and took his section, including Kelly, into a section of trench that had not been revetted. It is likely that the men had been forbidden to enter this trench during a bombardment. The account is instructive as it allows a comparison to be made between an officer's letter to a bereaved family and an eye-witness narrative:

> A little later, a 5.9" (shell) or two landed on top of the high parapet of that part of the trench, which collapsed and buried the entire section suffocating them.[21]

Private John Kelly. Image
courtesy of the *Blackburn Times*.

Private John Kelly has no known grave and is remembered on the Tyne Cot Memorial.

The battalion was in touch with the Menin Road, at the extreme left of the division. 'A' and 'B' Companies held the front line in front of Tower Hamlets ridge, while 'C' and 'D' Companies held the support line west of the crest. Numbers were again low in the battalion and reinforcements had a torrid time covering the ground already described by Milton Riley. Indeed, 'A' Company was down to fewer than thirty men in all. Many of the new drafts had been combed out of the Medical Corps, Veterinary Corps and Army Service Corps as a result of the manpower shortage that affected the Army at the end of 1917. Recruits who were often unsuited to front line service were pressed into action to fill the gaps at the front, as recruits began to dry up at the depots. These men were to suffer a disproportionately high number of casualties in the line owing to their inexperience and lack of training.

On the left of the East Lancashire position the Germans were barely forty yards away, though further distant on the right a pillbox known as Lewis House stood, the only landmark in an otherwise barren scene. Here the men stayed from 6 October, during which the rain poured, until 'C' and 'D' Companies took over the front line positions. So bad were the conditions that, in spite of well-practised precautions, trench foot began to take hold in the battalion:

> I surprised Cunliffe by asking for a supply of rum, which I did not like. (Riley had been brought up in a teetotal environment). He gave me a good supply of rum, and was watching to see that I didn't drink too much of it. I bathed my feet which felt numb in the nectar and wrapped them up in a trench coat 'fleece-lining' with which he obliged me. After a couple of hours I was all right again, except for the infection of depression.

The date 9 October brought the latest British offensive – the Battle of Poelcappelle. The divisions north of the Menin Road made the latest assault to take ground from the Germans, which ultimately resulted in failure. One barrage into the 37th Division positions lasted fourteen hours without cessation, turning the battlefield into a mass of shell holes with trenches and pillboxes in various conditions and the remnants of barbed wire and tree stumps. There was no escape for the men, who had only helplessly to endure.

A tank embedded in the mire, the salient, 1917.

Private George Ramsbottom. Image courtesy of the *Blackburn Times*.

8th Battalion veteran Thomas Heap remembered this time from the viewpoint of the 1980s:

It was here that we encountered the worst conditions I had experienced throughout the war. We had to hold the line for several days and all the time we were crawling in slutch. It was so bad we were unable to fire our rifles. The trenches were full of water and mud, with troops standing in them up to their armpits. Many deliberately laid on the top, even though under constant fire, with threat from shells, shrapnel, rifle and machine gun bullets. Here we did spells in and out of the front line. I was used mainly as a runner carrying messages to and from company to Battalion HQ along the Menin Road. Combined with this I was travelling with ration parties and relief parties to the front lines.

The battalion were due to be relieved on 10 October, but the company replacing 'A' Company became lost and could not get through in the morning, arriving only the following afternoon. The battalion was without rations and the effect was noticed even among the officers:

Ex-Sergeant Baker DCM, MM asked what was on our minds, and Cunliffe told him 'No breakfast!' Baker cheerfully picked up an empty sand tray and said 'I'll soon get you some breakfast, Sir!' And he did bringing with him a Father Christmas bag with all we could desire, Machonichie bully beef, bread, butter, tinned milk, jam, tea and sugar.[22]

Baker had emptied the canteen and haversacks of the unburied dead from around the position.

Later, on 11 October, 'A' Company was relieved and led by guides through the Dumbarton Woods area, only to become lost once more. Finding themselves deep in mud, with dusk coming on, the men took to the nearby Menin Road. Such was their exhaustion that one young soldier could not go on and only the Sergeant-Major flinging the whole of his kit into the mire induced him to do so. The Menin Road was habitually a dangerous route to take, but on this occasion the men were able to reach their camp at Fermoy Farm.

This photograph was taken when the 8th East Lancs were out of the line prior to the Passchendaele campaign and features scouts and runners with thier officer. Private Thomas Heap is pictured standing second from the left. Image courtesy of Joe Heap.

One of the last casualties of the 8th East Lancs' time in front of Gheluvelt was Private George Ramsbottom. The twenty-eight-year-old foundry worker from Blackburn was hit by a bullet on 11 October, dying the following day, and was buried at Locre Hospice Military Cemetery. A touching letter from an unknown comrade in the *Blackburn Times* underlined the close relationships formed in adversity:

My dear friends – I have received your letters and it is obvious from reading them that you are extremely upset. I can quite understand your feelings and you have my heartfelt sympathy. I am a soldier with a heart of steel, hardened with the horrors of war, but when I lost my friend the heart of steel was completely changed. I could not sleep that fatal night and ever since poor 'Ramie' has been on my mind, making me dejected and utterly miserable. Had he been my own brother I could not have worried more. 'Ramie' I can truthfully say, was one of the most popular men in the regiment. There was something about him that made us all like him. There were two other men killed the same day, but little was said of them, as they were not as well known as 'Ramie'. It was all poor 'Ramie'. Without a doubt there are loved ones left behind by the other two. My friend was buried the afternoon after he died, in a grave with two others of the same regiment … As a rule no burial service is read, as it is not practicable in this wicked war, but things being quiet, a chaplain came up and read the burial service … I despatched your husband's belongings the day after my last letter to you. The pipe, you will notice, is broken. He had it in his lower jacket pocket, and it was broken by the same bullet. I think that caused the bullet to turn, and instead of its going point forward, it entered the body lengthways, making a much larger wound than is usual with a bullet, thereby making the chance of recovery a remote one … I close, hoping that you will bear your troubles like your husband would have wished, that is, like a brave English woman.[23]

What was left of the village of Passchendaele was captured by the Canadians in mid-November, bringing a halt to one of the most controversial of campaigns of the First World War. The 8th East Lancashire gained battle honours for the Pilckem Ridge assault and their time in the line during the drive on Poelcappelle. They were to be the last of the war.

THE LAST DAYS OF THE BATTALION – 1918

The Winter of 1917–18

For the remainder of 1917, the 8th East Lancs passed their time parading, training and in working parties. There were short trench tours of the line south of the salient, as before, or in the vicinity of Hill 60. Out of the line, the much-frequented Wakefield Camp at Locre became their home. From a total of about 100 all ranks, when leaving Tower Hamlets, the addition of new arrivals brought the battalion up to the full strength of almost 900. The drafts were a mixed bunch, combining further groups of Army Service Corps and Veterinary Corps men with Class A4 recruits – soldiers under nineteen who would have been A1 if they had been nineteen years of age, but who had been sent to the front prematurely. More widely, the flow of reinforcements sent from the UK was thinning at the end of 1917.

Going the opposite way were twenty men who, prior to enlistment, had been ploughmen. They were sent back to the UK in mid-November, a sign that Britain needed to produce more food at home in the face of an aggressive U-Boat campaign.

In the summer of 1916, Guy Chapman imaginatively described his own 37th Division Battalion (13th Royal Fusiliers) in comparison with the one that had sailed at the end of July 1915. It was an appropriate comparison with which to describe the 8th East Lancashire in 1917:

> It was like an ancient garment which had been darned and redarned until, though it hangs in the same shape, few fragments of the original cloth remain. Here and there were patches of the first fabric. The transport, the stores, the orderly room still showed familiar faces. The RSM still swelled his chest and roared, though in a voice hoarser than of old … In the ranks appeared now and again a face one remembered, a Crossley, a Ting.[1]

The only officer remaining of those who had embarked with the battalion at Boulogne over two years earlier was Captain Bentley. He had risen slowly through the officer ranks, becoming the mainstay of the battalion. Little is known about Bentley, except that he attended Dulwich College during his youth, and after the war became captain of the Brighton Rugby Club, where, during his long association with the team, he was considered something of a character. Milton Riley gives a few hints to the type of man with the qualities of endurance possessed by someone who was witness to the countless deaths of his contemporaries. Following a leave late in 1917, Riley returned to the battalion with a gramophone player and a few records:

The mainstay of the 8th East Lancs – Captain Bentley, who served with the Battalion from the beginning of its time in France until it was disbanded in February 1918. Image courtesy of the Imperial War Museum, London. Ref. 0677/1. Also Mr Tom Yuille.

His (Bentley's) favourite record on the 'Decca' was not the song from 'Chu, Chin, Chow' – 'Any Time's Kissing Time.' He loathed it. So we usually put it on for him. One day he attempted to purloin it, and in the struggle, the precious record was smashed. 'Well,' he said, 'I've seen the last of that!' We broke it up that night into many small fragments which we placed in his 'flea-bag' (sleeping bag)

One of Captain Bentley's famous phrases was, 'Well,' as we set off on a 'Tour', 'off we go again, among the shit, the shot and the shell!'[2]

Christmas 1917 was spent out of the trenches and as January dawned, so too did rumours of a reorganisation of the British Army.

Disbanded

On 24 November 1917, Sir Douglas Haig advised the War Office that, unless more troops were forthcoming, he would have to break up fifteen of his fifty-seven divisions to bring the remaining formations back up to strength. The Cabinet committee on manpower disagreed; it proposed a reduction from twelve infantry battalions to nine in every division. The military members of the Army Council protested against this move, which affected every regiment of infantry and cut through an organisational structure for which every officer and man had been trained, but to no avail. The Army moved to the nine battalion structure in early 1918 and was still coming to terms with its effects well into the year.[3]

In 112 Brigade, the reorganisation demanded that three of its battalions be broken up – 11 Royal Warwicks, 10th Loyal North Lancs and 8th East Lancs. It was not considered right to disband regular and first-line territorial battalions. The brunt of the disbandment fell on the Service Battalions of Kitchener's Army, because of their low seniority. Hence, both the 7th and 8th Battalions of the East Lancashire Regiment were to be broken up.

The King's Colour of the 8th (Service) Battalion of the East Lancashire Regiment during 1914–18, on display at St Bartholomew's church in Colne.

Although Milton Riley had only been with the 8th Battalion since June, the news of the disbandment was a cause for gloom, though for veterans of the battalion such as Bentley, it must have been especially hard to accept.

> I asked Reynolds to ask the CO if I could join the unit in which was my elder brother Harold. The prospect of going to a lot of complete strangers in some other regiment did not appeal to me, and Harold wrote to me to say that his CO was willing to have me in his unit.[4]

The date 4 February 1918 was the official day allotted for the battalion's disbandment. The war diary is silent upon their passing, yet it was also the final day for 10th Loyals. A few days previously, the latter had entrained for the final time, as their battalion history and war diary commented:

> Before moving off there was a very special and mournful parade, when the battalion buried with all honours, the Flag that it had carried during so many years of war and through so many trying times. The ceremony ended with the CO delivering a speech of farewell to all ranks.[5]

> In spite of the heavy blow that has fallen on them, officers, non-commissioned officers and men have voiced with one accord their determination to uphold the good traditions of the battalion in whatever Regiment or Corps they may be called upon to serve.[6]

No doubt sentiments were similar in the East Lancashires. Altogether, the break-up took over three weeks and was completed in a number of stages. First to leave was a contingent of 400 men and twenty officers to the 11th East Lancs. Captain Bentley was placed in charge, accompanied by Captain Fleischer and a number of other officers. These men were replacements for the Accrington Pals and a few would go onto perform deeds of bravery. Captain Bentley was among them, winning an MC. CSM Fleming added a Warrant Officer's MC to the DCM he had won at Hook Trench. Fleischer himself won a DSO in the same sector as Fleming gained his award in June 1918. Many of the officers left behind headed for the base camp at Etaples, waiting to be reassigned to a new unit. The majority, including Riley, were to join the 2nd East Lancs, a regular battalion, which was a relief to many. He was to survive the war.

We felt pleased that we had not been drafted with the detachment to the 15th Entrenching Battalion that had been formed in the 37th Division. Sorry though we were that the 8th Battalion had been split up, those of us from HQ and the companies, who waited through the early months of March 1918, that fateful month, had still a strong sense of unity.[7]

15th Entrenching Battalion

Since the last quarter of 1917, Sir Douglas Haig knew that Germany had one last chance to seize the initiative on the Western Front. Russia had concluded a peace with the Kaiser, releasing many divisions from the Eastern Front. American forces would not be substantially deployed in the field until March 1918 at the earliest, while the French were content to wait upon their newest allies. British troop numbers were well below establishment during the final months of the Passchendaele Campaign, leading to the reorganisation of their divisions, as we have seen. From the beginning of 1918, the British and their allies were on the back foot for the first time since the beginning of the war. Building on what the Germans themselves had learned about fighting defensively, the British Army attempted to adopt a deep defensive zone, rather than a continuous trench line system.

The 15th Entrenching Battalion referred to by Riley absorbed the remainder, not only of the East Lancs men, but also the residues of the other disbanded battalions from 112 Brigade. The entrenching battalions were placed under Army or Corps control and were to be used on defensive work only, well behind the front line. Yet many of those 8th Battalion men who joined the 15th Entrenching Battalion were to be killed or captured during March 1918. Their deaths occurred so soon after the battalion's disbandment that they were listed as having died with it.

The date 21 March 1918 saw the great German offensive, largely against the British Fifth Army. For a time it drove the Allies back almost beyond Amiens and to the verge of defeat. During the opening days this battalion was heavily involved in defending against the German attacks in the area east of Peronne, near to Roisel, while in support to the 66th (East Lancashire) Division. They were then ordered to dig a new defensive line further back four days later. After a stubborn defence, the 15th Entrenching Battalion, along with the 66th Division, was all but destroyed by the end of March.

Among those captured was Private Alexander Brown, a forty-seven-year-old member of the original battalion who had enlisted in September 1914. As an older man, he may have been a member of the stores or transport section of the 8th Battalion. He was taken prisoner on 22 March, but died in German-held Valenciennes in August. He is buried in the cemetery there.[8] Other longstanding members of the battalion suffered a similar fate. At the end of April, the entrenching battalions had all been disbanded, their soldiers dispersed to rebuild the shattered units of the BEF. The last remnants of the 8th East Lancashire had gone. And so it was

Private Alexander Brown. Image courtesy
of the Denis Otter Collection.

that those men who had fought with the battalion ended the war with other units. There was
no formal ending, and the identity of a unit through which perhaps over 3,000 men might
have passed in 1914–18 began to die away.

For many soldiers, the Armistice signalled an end to the only life that they had known and
their futures suddenly opened up before them, creating expectations for a future for which
they had been fighting. Much of the disillusionment with the war came not in 1919, but later,
when 'a land fit for heroes' failed to materialise.

Unemployment greeted many of those leaving the Army who had left to enlist in 1914–15
and beyond. Promises to hold open jobs for the duration had been broken in the face of a
severe economic downturn in the opening years of the 1920s, caused by the enormous debts
created by the war. Many had been physically and mentally scarred and the number of towns
and villages without a destitute soldier wandering their streets were few.

Others became disillusioned with their treatment by employers, unable to take advantage
of the confidence, experience and skills gained in war. Soldiers were often alienated from the
very people for whom they had been fighting, some of whom they perceived to have gained
by being at home. Milton Riley, writing in the late 1960s, quoted an American acquaintance of
Churchill to illustrate his feelings:

> I have always resented the consignments of military men to the status of second class citizens
> in time of peace – most of the military minds I have met have been top-notch, the kind that
> would permit a man to succeed in any field …

Riley added bitterly:

> … But seldom in a 'Rat Race' among gangs of civilians, professional, industrial or commercial;
> or trade union gangsters and looters.[9]

Colonel Spencer Richard Fleischer CBE DSO
MC. Image courtesy of Anthony Fleischer.

CSM James Fleming also became disheartened after the war. Deciding to stay in the Army,
he was transferred to 2nd Battalion East Lancs, which was stationed in Ireland. Unhappy with
what he saw as the mistreatment of the Irish, he left the Army in 1920, returning to the pit at
Atherton he had left six years earlier. Initially, the owners offered the double medal winner and
local hero a job as their chauffeur. Eventually however, Fleming was reduced to cleaning the
pit baths, unable to resume work down the pit because of the wounds he had suffered. For a
former Warrant Officer and holder of a MC and DCM, this was difficult to bear, made worse
by his family's increasing poverty during the Miners' Strike in the autumn of 1926. At this
lowest ebb, Fleming supported his family of six children by the illegal practice of scavenging
coal from local slag heaps, becoming an admirer of the Communist ideal and an active union
member in the process. Things improved little during the years of the Depression in the 1930s,
yet Fleming brought up his family with pride and dignity. At the onset of the Second World
War, he enlisted once more, principally to augment the family's income, joining the Infantry
Training Centre of the East Lancashire Regiment at Blackpool, where he was able to put his
skills and experience to better use. Fleming's increased salary and the family's receipt of the
United Services Fund helped to raise the family out of poverty and create a better future for
his wife and children.

Numerous First World War veterans like James Fleming eagerly volunteered for service in the
Second World War, holding positions of responsibility, often involved in training and providing
the backbone of the Home Guard.

Yet there were those too for whom the war had been a great adventure, a time that they
looked on in later life as one of excitement and comradeship when, in spite of the dangers and
suffering, everything that followed in the rest of their lives was almost anticlimactic.

Many used their experiences to launch new careers and to put the skills they had learned
at war to new use in peace. One such was the South African officer Spencer Fleischer, of the
contingent drafted from the 8th to the Pals:

Fleischer rose through the mining profession in South Africa; deeply involved in the discovery of the Far West Rand Goldfields, he ultimately became President of the Transvaal and Orange Free State Chamber of Mines in 1951. He raised the Mines Engineering Brigade at the outbreak of the Second World War, and in 1940 was appointed to its command with the rank of Lieutenant-Colonel. In 1946, he was appointed Honorary Colonel of the Imperial Light Horse.[10]

Regimental reunions flourished during the twenties and thirties when, for a short time, a veteran could renew acquaintance with others who understood. Yet, while reunions and the close geographical proximity of recruitment sustained the veterans of the Accrington Pals into the future, the memory of many of the Service Battalions simply faded away. There is no evidence for a formal reunion of the 8th East Lancashire. No doubt small numbers who had enlisted locally together or fought side by side met on occasions, while others attended general regimental functions at Fulwood Barracks. For the majority, however, the memory of the 'Galloping 8th' slowly faded.

Now all its members have gone. The year 2014 will see the hundredth anniversary of the formation of the 8th East Lancashire. By then, the publication of this book and others like it may be seen as timely, for with the passing of the veterans and their children too, perhaps the memory of and interest in the First World War will begin to fade also.

8

CEMETERIES, BATTLEFIELDS, MEMORIALS – WHAT TO SEE TODAY

Ninety years have now passed since the end of the First World War. In the UK, France and Belgium, it is still possible to stand where the soldiers of the 8th Battalion of the East Lancashire Regiment stood and to gain an impression of what they saw. This chapter highlights places mentioned in this book that are still possible to visit by car and on foot. It is not exhaustive, merely reflecting the authors' own research and interest.

What follows is not a comprehensive tour; there are many such books that do that successfully. Nor are many of the places described below included in the itinerary of the many commercial tour companies. However, some indication is given in the text of how to gain the best viewing points. It is important to stress that in a few places the landscape has changed beyond recognition. However, by using a trench map and with some background reading, it is possible to walk the ground and gain a greater understanding of where the 8th Battalion fought and died.

Suggestions for Battlefield Walkers in France and Belgium

The weather in Picardy, Artois and Flanders can be excellent, though it can be changeable and carrying wet weather clothing is essential. So too is stout footwear. Trench maps can be ordered from the Western Front Association and the relevant French Ordnance Map (IGN) is advisable. Water bottles and small first aid kits are indispensable items! Walkers expecting regularly to come across cafés and shops for refreshments will be disappointed. Many of the geographical features are referred to by the names they were given by the British during the war – for example, Dumbarton Lakes.

The battlefields of the First World War are, for the most part, to be found in fields devoted to agriculture. Many farmers, though by no means all, are used to battlefield visitors, though straying into open fields, woods and copses should be avoided. Walkers should stick to tracks, though some stop suddenly in the middle of fields. As in the UK, however, locals will not welcome visitors trampling crops or trespassing. When parking in France, take care not to block paths or roads used by agricultural machinery. Watch out for signs marked 'la chasse' during the hunting season in France, the late summer and autumn. Not everyone with a gun has safety in mind!

Many local people will go out of their way to help if they can. On the Loos battlefield, the authors' trench map attracted the attention of five locals, resulting in the correct orientation of the map and a personal tour of the museum at Loos! Learning a few words of French is really helpful in this respect, and much appreciated by those you meet, though generally to be avoided in the Flemish-speaking part of Belgium.

Above all, leave all old battlefield munitions where they are. People continue to be killed by the relics of the First World War to this day.

The Double-Crassier, close to Loos, as it is today from Vimy Ridge.

The hospital at Hazebrouck as it was when the authors visited in 1998, just prior to demolition. Ironically, the 8th East Lancs were billeted here in August 1915 when it was under construction. The hospital's archive records its use during 1914–18.

The headstone of Colour Sergeant C.W. Kent in Ludgershall churchyard. He died while attached to the 8th East Lancs.

What to see in England

Sites around Ludgershall, Wiltshire

On the southern edge of the village of Ludgershall can still be seen the remnants of the old railway platforms, now defunct, where King George V arrived to review the 37th Division. Another set of platforms, still in use on the western fringe, were those from where the 8th East Lancs departed for Folkestone on 31 July 1915. In the churchyard can be found the Commonwealth War Graves Commission (CWGC) headstone of Colour Sergeant C.W. Kent, who died while attached to the 8th Battalion from the National Rifle Association School of Musketry. He was fifty-six years old and from Cricklewood in London.

Windmill Hill today. Tents would have lined these slopes over ninety years ago.

The Windmill Hill site, where the 8th Battalion camped during training, is a quarter of an hour's walk from the centre of Ludgershall, to the west of the village. The bare lower slopes rising to a wooded crest were covered with the battalion's tents. Drive to Tidworth and then north along the A338. A few hundred yards after leaving Tidworth take a wide rough track on the left leading up to Sidbury Hill, where King George V inspected the 37th Division. Near the top on the right is a natural bowl surrounded by wooded slopes. It was in this vale that the inspection took place.

What to see in France

The village of Nielles-les-Ardres

On the nights of 2–3 August 1915, the first billets in a French village were found for the battalion in this village. Nielles-les-Ardres lies approximately twenty miles from Calais on the N43, in the direction of St Omer. Turn left off the main road into the village and park close to the Mairie. Opposite is a green, an ideal spot for a picnic. Almost 900 men of the battalion were billeted in the barns around the village. The church and cemetery are interesting to explore and, while doing so, ponder the thoughts of those travelling abroad to war.

Drive north-west past the calvary, into Rue de Meraville. Here you will find the small chateau and its outbuildings used by both 112 Brigade and the 8th East Lancs. The owner of the chateau was helpful during our visit, explaining that during the Second World War it was occupied by the Germans, who began construction of a V1 site in the grounds behind.

A view of the 8th East Lancs' position on the Foncquevillers battlefield today. This image was taken from the British side of the line, close to the Brayelle road. The slopes of the German position can clearly be seen. The hedge line on the right marks the approximate position of the 'Z'. The North Fortin was beyond the pylon, the South Fortin to the right of the photograph down the slope. The British front-line trenches are marked by the electricity cables on their north-south alignment.

Foncquevillers

Foncquevillers is a commune in the Pas-de-Calais département. It lies at the northern end of the 1 July 1916 front line. The 8th East Lancashire held the line here from September 1915 to May 1916. Take the road on the south side of the church towards the eastern edge of the settlement. Turn left at the calvary and follow the road up to the next junction. Here, park safely and climb the bank to look out over the open ground. Behind you in the trees was 'Snipers' Square'. Two companies of 8th East Lancs were often in dugouts in reserve here.

Looking east, a line of electricity pylons can be seen. These mark the approximate line of the battalion's sector of the front line. The left company front ran roughly opposite the line from the poplars on the left through the 'Big' and 'Little' 'Zs'. The right company front curved round to face Gommecourt Wood. If 'B' Company held this latter part of the line in December, as they had two months earlier, then it is on this ground that Private William Young won his VC.

Go back through the village to Foncquevillers Military Cemetery. All the East Lancashires buried here are from the 8th Battalion. Use the cemetery register to find 17258 Private Smith, 17146 Lance-Corporal Everett and 16156 Corporal Robertson, buried next to each other in Plot I, Row J. All three were killed by an accidental grenade explosion on 3 May 1916.

St Amand

From Foncquevillers, drive a few miles westward to Souastre and continue on to St Amand. These two villages were frequently used by the 8th Battalion during their time out of the trenches. Behind the line they suffered relatively little damage and the type of farm buildings and barns used to house the men are still to be seen. Cruck frame barns, with their plaster coverings, would have been familiar, as would those farms surrounded by a courtyard, often home to Company or Battalion HQ.

At the crossroads in St Amand, turn left into the Rue du Four. After a short distance, stop before the arched entrance to the farm owned by Pierre Tesserine. Monsieur Tesserine's mother ran the farm during the First World War and he claims that the large chalk barn to the right of the gate was used for concert parties, possibly by the 'Barn Owls'. Throughout its length it is covered in soldiers' graffiti, some of it by soldiers of the 37th Division.

The church and barns at St Amand today.

The venue, arguably, of the 'Barn Owls' performances at St Amand. The barn is owned by M. Pierre Tesserine.

Bienvillers au Bois

Return the short distance to Souastre and then follow directions to Bienvillers au Bois along the D2. After about three miles on the left, just before the village, is Bienvillers Military Cemetery. It was begun by the 37th Division in September 1915. There are two 8th Battalion men buried here: 16566 Private Shields from Liverpool, Plot XII, Row D, Grave 1 and the battalion's well-loved second-in-command, Major Magrath, Plot XII, Row C, Grave 1. Continue into the village and park opposite the church. The scene is little changed after ninety years. The 8th Battalion had a canteen in Bienvillers, a wooden hut erected close to the church. Lieutenant Macqueen was forced to evacuate it as he was stocktaking during a brief bombardment in May 1916.

The centre of Bienvillers as it is today.

Bienvillers centre as it was when the 8th East Lancs were billeted there from time to time. The battalion's wooden canteen was erected close to this church.

The Battle of the Somme, 1916

From the centre of Albert, take the D929 towards Bapaume. The battalion marched up this road on 3 July 1916. Park at Bapaume Post Military Cemetery on the right of the road. From here you have the panoramic view of the 1 July front line, described in the 8th Battalion's war diary – Ovillers to the left, La Boisselle straight ahead and the Lochnagar mine crater to the right.

Continue to La Boisselle and then take the road to Bécourt. The battalion camped in the rear of Bécourt Wood, getting soaked in the pouring rain on the night of 3 July 1916. In the atmospheric Military Cemetery there are the remains of six men of the battalion, including Private John Hall, who had returned from America to enlist, in Plot I Row R Grave 7. These men had been killed or wounded between Bécourt and Contalmaison and sent back to the nearby chateau turned hospital.

Pozières – 15 July 1916

To visit the site of the battalion's attack, go to La Boisselle and take the road to Contalmaison. Just before the village pass Bailiff Wood on the right, and then almost immediately turn left on the D147 towards the village of Pozières. After about 100 yards, park safely on the left just before Contalmaison Wood. A walk around the battlefield takes approximately two hours.

The East Lancs covered the ground in front of you, roughly from Bailiff to Contalmaison Wood, their trees mere stumps at this time. Continue on foot along the road towards Pozières, mounting the bank on the left after the wood. Here you can see the ground of the attack up to Pozières, with its church spire visible above the trees. You can estimate the position on the rise where the Germans opened fire on the 112 Brigade.

Carry on to the village, imagining the scene on your left, as 1,100 men of the brigade became casualties. The Germans held the fringe of the village marked roughly by the

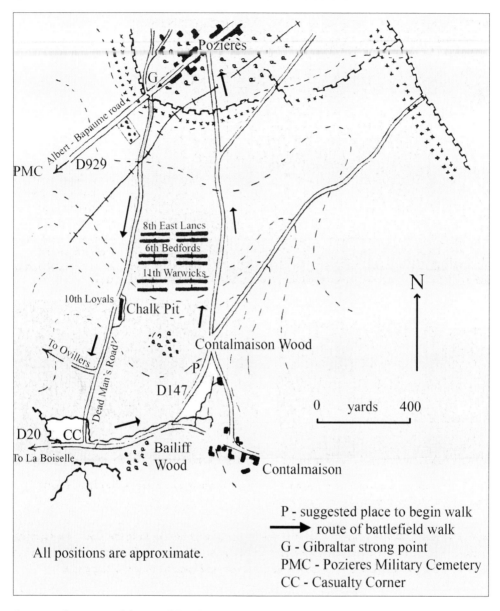

A suggested tour around the site of the 8th East Lancashire attack on Pozières, 15 July 1916.

modern-day orchards. Cross the main road and visit the Gibraltar strong point – its machine-gunners pouring fire into the Lancastrians. You will get a good impression from the viewing platform here.

Go back across the main road and walk briefly towards Albert, taking the first left turn down a farm track known as 'Dead Man's Road'. Continue with the battlefield now on your left until you come to the Chalk Pit. Here officers of various battalions converged, along with Major-General Ingouville-Williams, GOC 34th Division. Many of the wounded were brought here. Carry on along the track noticing an exposed dugout in the tree line on the left.

Just before you come to the La Boisselle-Contalmaison Road, carefully walk up the rise of the overgrown bank on the right. This was the position occupied by the advanced dressing

The remains of the Gibraltar Point position at Pozières. Its machine guns raked the 8th East Lancs as they left the sheltered ground beyond Contalmaison Wood.

Left: The Chalk Pit, south of Pozières. *Right:* A dugout photographed recently in Dead Man's Road, close to the Chalk Pit on the Pozières battlefield.

station called 'Casualty Corner'. The wounded were brought back along the track you have just walked. Look back over the battlefield and consider the distance the battalion had to cover to achieve its objective. Turn left towards Contalmaison and back to your starting point.

The Pozières Military Cemetery

Drive to Pozières Military Cemetery on the main Albert–Bapaume Road. Eighteen men of the East Lancashire, killed on 15 July, are buried here, with a further sixty-five commemorated on the Thiepval Memorial. 6238 Private Herbert Gavin, from Burnley, was rewarded while training at Plymouth for saving a man from drowning. His burial place can be found in Plot III, Row F, Grave 30. The bodies of a few of these men were recovered long after the battle, but before the end of the war.

Redan Ridge – 15 November 1916

Mailly-Maillet

The battalion visited this village on several occasions. Before visiting the Redan Ridge battlefield, follow directions on the D919 towards Serre. Just as you leave Mailly-Maillet, on

The remains of the windmill just outside Mailly-Maillet. It was from this point that the 8th East Lancs began the journey that ended with the attack on Redan Ridge on 15 November 1916.

the left you will see the mound of the old windmill next to the road. It was from here that 2nd Division guides rendezvoused with the East Lancashires and Loyals to take them to the front. To your right front is Redan Ridge. The men travelled up communication trenches covering the ground on the right of the road, taking five hours in the dark, foggy, congested and mud-ridden conditions.

Redan Ridge

For those wishing to visit the scene of the battalion's attack of 15 November 1916, make for Beaumont Hamel. In the centre of the village follow the signs for Waggon Road and Munich Trench Cemeteries. As you ascend gently onto Redan Ridge, a high bank develops on the right. You are now at the point on Waggon Road where many of the battalion and 10th Loyals took cover during the attack on Frankfurt and Munich Trenches.

Go into Waggon Road Cemetery on the right and look west towards the edge of the ridge. The two towers of Serre Cemetery No 2 are visible. The attack of 8th East Lancashire and 10th Loyals began from Beaumont Trench, roughly three-quarters of the way across the ridge. The field was thick with mud and fog filled the air. Many of the men were driven to your left down the gentle slope towards Beaumont Hamel, taking cover behind the bank in Waggon Road, which is just visible.

Munich Trench itself ran behind the cemetery to your right front, about 100 yards away and from which the cemetery got its name. It passed about 150 yards behind where you are now, in Waggon Road Cemetery, and headed away east of the two other cemeteries on this part of the ridge, Frankfurt and New Munich Trench. The line of Frankfurt Trench itself was 200 yards further east still. These four small cemeteries mentioned are some of the most beautiful in the Somme area and the burials there are of men killed close by.

In Waggon Road Cemetery are the graves of eighteen men of the battalion. The men are recorded as having died here on 16 November. They had, in fact, died the day previously, as

Above: Munich Trench Cemetery.

Left: The grave of Private Huyton in Munich Trench. His moving epitaph reads: *No word of comfort could he have from those who loved him most.*

all primary sources indicate. The battalion lost ten officers that day, many of whom had only recently joined from reserve battalions. Four are buried here, notably seventeen-year-old 2nd Lieutenant Eddie Fisher, one of the youngest officers killed in the Somme battles, and 2nd Lieutenant Minaar, a South African from Cape Province.

Go back to the road and carry on to Munich Trench Cemetery. Here there are fourteen East Lancashire casualties of the action. Another South African officer, 2nd Lieutenant Morkel, lies here, as does 23578 Private Huyton from Preston. Huyton's grave has inscribed at its base one of the most moving epitaphs of any:

No word of comfort could he have from those who loved him well.

There was little comfort on the Redan Ridge.

The memorial to the 37th Division, Monchy-le-Preux.

The Battles of Arras 1917
Arras

The Arras Memorial is in the Faubourg-d'Amiens Cemetery, which is in the Boulevard du General de Gaulle in the western part of the town of Arras. The cemetery is near the Citadel, approximately two kilometres due west of the railway station. It is a good place to begin, as over 120 men of the 8th Battalion with no known grave are remembered here – that is over one-fifth of their total dead in the First World War. The majority were killed in the fighting close to Monchy-le-Preux and Gavrelle during April and May 1917. The East Lancashire missing are inscribed in Bay 6.

Monchy-le-Preux

From Arras, take the D939 towards Cambrai. As you near Monchy-le-Preux, you are following the line of the East Lancashire attacks running along the left of the road towards the village during 9–11 April 1917. As you pass over the A1 motorway, take a moment to stop, taking in the view of Monchy. The fields during this period were covered in snow and cavalry and tanks manoeuvred over the ground.

Continue on until reaching Windmill Cemetery, found about 150 yards from the left turn into the D33 (Hussar Lane), towards Monchy itself. After parking, pass along the front of the stones to face westwards in the direction of Arras. During 10 and 11 April, the East Lancashire was heading directly towards you and five of their dead are buried in graves close by (Hayes, Metcalfe, Entwistle, Neil and Riding). The men dug in around the lane behind, along with 3rd Dragoon Guards and other cavalry units. It was along this narrow road that the battalion repulsed German counterattacks and suffered a heavy bombardment during 11 April.

Windmill Cemetery, just south of Monchy-le-Preux. On 10–11 April 1917, the 8th East Lancs advanced directly towards the camera, close to the Arras-Cambrai Road.

Next, drive up to the village, ignoring the road as it winds to the right, continuing straight on into the Rue de Chaussy. After 100 yards, turn sharply left into the Rue de Tilloy. Immediately on your right is the 37th Division Memorial.

The memorial was officially unveiled early in October 1921 by the French General Debeney, who was welcomed by Major-General Lord Edward Gleichen, GOC 37th Division. His successor, Major-General Sir H. Bruce-Williams, was also in attendance with a large party of veterans. The monument itself had been sculpted by Lord Gleichen's sister Feodora, who was also present.[1]

The Action at Hook Trench – The night of 30–31 May 1917

This action is best viewed on foot, the following walk taking around two hours. Leaving your car in the centre of Monchy, head south-east along the Rue de Vis. After passing the last residential house on the left, continue on for another 200 yards and then turn left onto a farm track. Walk about 400 yards until the track bends gently to the right and then stop. The large wood on the rise in front of you is the Bois du Vert, a spot popular with German artillery observers. In the field to your left front is an electricity pylon. This marks the approximate line of Hook Trench as it ran parallel to the Bois de Vert and the ridge. To your right in the field about 200 yards away is a small copse. The jumping-off line for the 8th East Lancs was Hill Trench, which ran on a north-south axis parallel to Hook Trench, approximately in line with the western end of the copse. The block in Tool Trench taken by the battalion that night is roughly 150 yards from the north-eastern face of the copse. Captain Forster was killed in Hook Trench, probably in the fields to your left, and it was in this area also that CSM Fleming won the DCM.

Look back into Monchy and consider the distance gained between the capture of Monchy on 11 April and this action. The short distance tells something of the ferocity of the fighting in the area.

Passing just south of the Bois du Vert, continue along the track, turning sharply right onto the Rue de Guemappe. After 800 yards, turn right, back into the Rue de Vis and return to Monchy. When the authors last visited this area in 2006 there were many unexploded Stokes Mortar round in the fields, testament to the type of warfare that went on here.

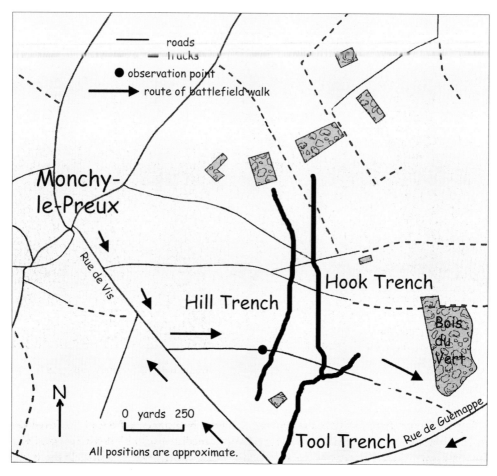

Putting yourself on the spot – the attack on Hook Trench, east of Monchy-le-Preux by the 8th East Lancs during the night of 30–31 May 1917.

What to See in Belgium

The Battles of 3rd Ypres – 31 July to mid-November 1917
The Menin Gate – Ypres

Twenty-one members of the 8th East Lancashire are remembered here, along with 54,300 other soldiers missing in the Ypres salient prior to 16 August 1917. Those whose bodies were never found after this date have their names inscribed on the Tyne Cot Memorial. Twenty of the battalion were killed in the attack on Rifle Farm on 31 July, the first day of the battle. Among them on panel 34 is 37639 Private Robert Ashworth from Blackburn. Ashworth had been Milton Riley's runner during the latter's first trench tour.

Tyne Cot Memorial – Zonnebeke

Almost 35,000 missing soldiers are commemorated on the walls of the largest Commonwealth War Graves Commission Cemetery at Tyne Cot. These men were killed from 16 August onwards, with thirty-eight 8th Battalion soldiers remembered on panels 77–79. Among them

Veteran Thomas Heap during his pilgrimage to the Tyne Cot Memorial and Cemetery in the 1980s. Image courtesy of Joe Heap.

is Captain Dmitri Jarintzoff MC, shot through the head by a sniper in front of Gheluvelt on 10 October. Milton Riley attended Jarintzoff's body immediately after his death. Jarintzoff was the son of an émigré Russian general and his wife Nadine, who wrote extensively about her native country and was an avid spiritualist. Their son read science at Merton College, Oxford, before being employed by Messers Brunner & Mond at their Winnington Works factory, near Northwich in Cheshire. At the outbreak of war, Jarintzoff joined a battalion of the London Regiment, rising to CSM and was then commissioned into the East Lancashire Regiment. His name is first mentioned in the battalion history in connection with the attack on Redan Ridge in November 1916.

Milton Riley also mentions 37128 Private John Kelly from Blackburn, with whose mother Riley's family exchanged letters. He was nineteen years old. No 8th East Lancs men are buried in the vast cemetery at Tyne Cot.

Visiting the Area Behind the Lines

Locre and Kemmel

From Ypres, take the N331 to Dranoutre and from there the road to Locre. This is a journey of about nine miles. As you approach Locre, you are encircled by the Flanders Hills, from Kemmel in the east to Mont Noir in the west. Just south of Locre, on the left-hand side of the road from Dranoutre, is a valley. Park the car on the right-hand side and cross the road to a number of allotments overlooking the valley. At its bottom, ninety years ago, was a wooded area in which was a large hutted camp called Wakefield Huts by the British. The 8th Battalion spent many days here when out of the line during the summer and autumn 1917. During August 1915 they spent their time digging trenches in the rear areas at Locre and Kemmel. They were back again almost two years later, barely recognisable as the same unit.

Locre Hospice Cemetery, the final resting place of Brigadier-General Maclachlan, GOC 112 Brigade.

There was a terrible reminder of the dangers of unexploded ammunition when, in October 2007, a Locre villager was killed in his garden by a large explosion from munitions he had gathered!

Climb gently into the village and then turn right in the direction of Kemmel. Approximately a mile from Locre on the road to Kemmel, visit Locre Hospice Cemetery. There are two 8th East Lancashire men buried here: 24700 Private Arthur Taylor, a thirty-year-old weaver from Burnley and 24916 Private George Ramsbottom, 'Ramie' to his mates, a very popular soldier, according to a letter in the *Blackburn Times* of 27 October 1917, quoted in chapter 6.

Also buried here is the much-admired GOC 112 Brigade, Brigadier-General Ronald Maclachlan, killed by a sniper during one of his regular tours of the front line in the Oostaverne sector.

Rifle Farm Assault – 31 July 1917

Only for those who enjoy a challenge, this sector is difficult to interpret and should only be undertaken with a trench map and war diary. However, as one of the least-visited battlefronts, it has its own rewards.

Leaving Ypres by the Lille Gate, drive south on the N365. After a couple of miles, take the N336 towards Oostaverne and Bas-Warneton. From this junction, and after about two-and-a-half miles, take the fifth turning on the left into an unobtrusive road called the Kaleutestraat. You are now into open pasture and the landscape is devoid of easily recognisable landmarks. After a hundred yards, the road bends to the right and straightens for a few hundred yards passing a left, then almost immediately a right junction in front of a farm. Pass them both until you come to a crossroads, parking safely at the corner. This crossroads was a fork junction in 1917 (map reference O.23.b.2.4 referred to in the war diary).

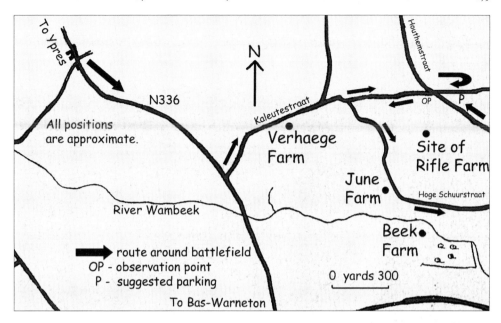

Visiting the site of the attack on Rifle Farm on 31 July 1917 is a challenge, but an interesting one. It is a rarely visited part of the Ypres battlefields.

From the corner, Rifle Farm was 200 yards due south of you in the middle of the field. Nothing remains of it as of October 2007. Its position is marked by a small wooden animal shelter, though the position of the old farm buildings is clear in aerial photographs. The line of Rifle Farm to the crossroads was the left of the 8th East Lancashire objective on 31 July. The battalion attacked from the direction of the farms south-west of your position, which is where to head next.

Return to your car and drive back the way you came, taking the first left turn after 400 yards. Follow this narrow track across the front of the battalion attack, remembering that ninety years ago the ground became heavily sodden in the pouring rain. It is easy to appreciate how difficult orientation must have been in such a landscape. As the road bends to the left, follow it past an elegant house and then stop in front of the next building on the right. This was June Farm, the objective on the right battalion front as the attack came in from the west.

Continue on for a short distance, following the road as it turns sharply left close to Beek Farm, in front of which are a pond and stream – the Wambeek, indicated on the map in the battalion history (p.440). Carry on to the T-junction and then turn left back to the crossroads where you began.

Opposite Gheluvelt 4–11 October 1917

Leave Ypres close to the Menin Gate and head south-east towards Menin on the N8. Drive for approximately four miles before parking alongside the main road close to thick woodland on your right, just before entering the village of Gheluvelt. Leave a couple of hours for this walk around the battlefield. Head for Gheluvelt on the southern side of the road. Once clear of the trees, continue on 150 yards and then turn right into Waterstraat. Continue on for another 550 yards up to a small crossroads. The road to your left is called Everzwijnhoekstraat, and for those with no trench map this very roughly marks the line of the trenches held by 112 Brigade units during their stay here from 4–11 October 1917. Those with a war diary can use the co-ordinates recorded there to pinpoint the exact trench position, south-east of this road. The area

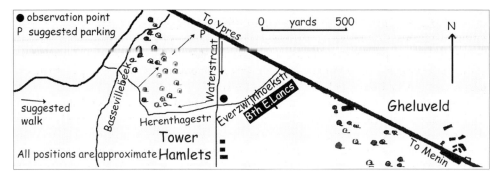

A suggested tour to the site of the 8th East Lancashire positions of 4–11 October 1917.

A typical pillbox in the salient of 1917. This one remains on Hill 60.

has been built over for the most part and visualising the trenches is not an easy task. It was in this position that Milton Riley witnessed the deaths of Captain Dmitri Jarintzoff and Private John Kelly. Their names are recorded on the Tyne Cot Memorial.

Return to the crossroads and go on along Waterstraat as before for a further 150 yards. Stand in front of a row of houses on the eastern side of the road. These buildings mark the German stronghold known as Tower Hamlets, consisting of a number of pillboxes. With the houses at your back, look west from your position on this high ground towards the trees – those on the right were called Bass Wood by the British. This wood has grown greater in size from east to west since the First World War, the western half marking part of the ground well known to the battalion as Dumbarton Lakes. Before you leave this point, imagine a different view from ninety years ago – a sea of mud and water-filled shell holes, through which ran ribbons of duckboard roads among the shattered remains of woodland. The land was punctuated by pillboxes, abandoned tanks, and detritus in all its forms.

At this point you can either return to your car or investigate the Dumbarton Lakes position. Go back to the crossroads and turn left down Tower Hamlets Ridge into Herenthagestraat. Walk for about half a mile, until the road turns sharply to the right. Stop here and find the line of the Bassevillebeek stream, which in its swollen state in 1917 presented a significant obstacle to the movement of casualties and reinforcements. To the west is Bodmin Copse and south of that Shrewsbury Forest. Continue up the road north for a short distance and then head into the wood on your right using one of the footpaths. This area of woodland has recently been opened to the public. The ground here among the trees is marshy, and is punctuated by ponds at various points and was part of the Dumbarton Lakes area, though the landscape has changed somewhat. Using the marked footpaths, make your way to the main road, the N8 and rejoin your car. This takes no longer than half an hour.

GLOSSARY

'A' Frames A basic structure designed to bear a load.

Artillery formation Single section or platoon files to avoid multiple casualties in the event of an artillery strike.

Bite and hold An assault in which the attacker hopes to occupy and then secure a limited portion of the defender's front line.

Bull Ring British Army training establishment, such as the base camp at Etaples, which was infamous for its severe discipline.

Corons (French) miners' cottages

Corps Line One of a series of defensive positions well behind the front line, to be manned in the event of an enemy breakthrough.

Estaminet Civilian run bar or café for off-duty soldiers on the Western Front.

GOC General Officer Commanding.

Green card A gallantry card recommended by a division to men whose actions were recommended to its officers.

GSO1 General Staff Officer.

Lachrymatory shells Shells filled with gas fired by artillery.

Maxim The first automatic machine gun ever invented, used by American forces and in 'modified' versions by Britain, Germany and Russia.

Minenwerfer The name for a class of short-range trench mortars (literally – 'mine launcher').

Revetted To reinforce the sides of a trench with supporting materials.

Swedish Drill Method of physical training involving drill routines.

Vermoral Sprayer A hand-pumped fire extinguisher filled with a sodium thiosulfate solution to neutralise residual chlorine gas in trenches.

Warrant Officer Senior non-commissioned officer in a class of their own between NCOs and commissioned officers.

REFERENCES

Introduction

1. Beattie, p.12

Chapter One

1. Simkins, p.195–6.
2. Simkins, p.173.
3. Simkins, p.107.
4. Simkins, p.175.
5. Wood (7KSLI History), p.206.
6. Simkins, p.243.
7. *Bournemouth Daily Echo*, 9 November 1914.
8. Nicholson and McMullen, p.405.
9. *Bournemouth Daily Echo*, 14 November 1914.
10. *The Bournemouth Graphic*, 20 November 1914.
11. *Bournemouth Daily Echo*, 14 November 1914.
12. Edgington, p.9.
13. Simkins, p.249.
14. Nicholson and McMullen, p.405.
15. Nicholson and McMullen, p.203.
16. *The Bournemouth Graphic*, 5 March 1915.
17. Simkins, p.249.
18. Putkowski.
19. *Golden Horseshoe*, p.14.
20. *Golden Horseshoe*, p.15.
21. Simkins, p.307.
22. *Golden Horseshoe*, p.15.
23. *Health and Strength*, 21 August 1915.
24. IWM, Johnstone, 02/29/1.
25. Nicholson and McMullen, p.406.
26. IWM, Mountford, 02/08/06.
27. IWM, Johnstone, 02/29/1.
28. Nicholson and McMullen, p.409.

Chapter Two

1. *Golden Horseshoe*, p.16.
2. Holding, p.58.
3. Van Emden and Humphries, p.50.
4. Nicholson and McMullen, p.412.
5. *Blackburn Times*, 2 October 1915.
6. *Blackburn Times*, 2 October 1915.
7. *Rossendale Free Press*, 2 October 1915.

8. National Archives WO95 2512 – 37th Division War Diary.
9. Fuller, p.58.
10. National Archives WO95 2535 – 112 Brigade War Diary.
11. IWM Buckeridge, 12127 04/39/1.
12. Chapman, p.46.
13. Nicholson and McMullen, p.414.
14. National Archives WO95 2537 – 8th East Lancs War Diary.
15. Kirby, p.6.
16. *Lancashire Daily Post*.
17. National Archives WO95 2512 – 37th ^Division War Diary.
18. National Archives WO95 2537 – 8th East Lancs War Diary.
19. Liddle Collection, Leeds University, ref. GS0840.
20. *Accrington Observer and Times*, 26 February 1916.
21. Liddle Collection, Leeds University, ref. GS0840.
22. Collinson, p.53.
23. *Golden Horseshoe*, p.65.
24. IWM Buckeridge, 12127 04/39/1.
25. Macdonald, p.90.
26. Macdonald, p.90.
27. National Archives WO95 2535 – 112 Brigade War Diary.
28. National Archives WO95 2512 – 37th Division War Diary.
29. Chapman, p.66.
30. IWM 10752 Misc 101 (1559).
31. *Farnworth Journal*, 11 August 1916.
32. Junger, p.82.
33. *Leigh Journal*, 14 July 1916.
34. Junger, p.82.

Chapter Three

1. Macdonald, p.92.
2. *Golden Horseshoe*, p.16.
3. Collinson, p.75.

4. IWM, Wilson MSS, Wilson diary, 11, 12 and 14 October 1916, quoted in *Haig's Generals*.
5. *Burnley Express*, 29 July 1916.
6. National Archives WO95 2432 – 34th Division War Diary.
7. Collinson, p.84.
8. National Archives WO95 673 – III Corps War Diary.
9. National Archives WO95 2432 – 34th Division War Diary.
10. National Archives WO95 2535/6 – 112 Brigade War Diary.
11. Nicholson and McMullen, p.423.
12. IWM Yuille, 15199 06/77/1.
13. Collinson, p.85.
14. Collinson, p.86.
15. *Burnley Express*, 16 September 1916.
16. National Archives WO95 2432 – 34th Division War Diary.
17. Collinson, p.87.
18. *Burnley Express*, 12 February 1916.
19. *Northwich Guardian*, 30 March 1917.
20. Crompton, p.173.
21. *Bolton Journal*, 4 August 1916.
22. Nicholson and McMullen, p.423.
23. National Archives WO95 2221 – 25th Division War Diary.
24. National Archives WO95 673 – III Corps War Diary.
25. National Archives WO95 2535/6 – 112 Brigade War Diary.
26. *Burnley News*, 6 September 1916.
27. Simkins, p.151.
28. Simkins, p.158.
29. Chapman, p.100.
30. National Archives WO95 2537 – 8th East Lancs War Diary.
31. *Blackburn Times*, 19 August 1916.
32. Nicholson and McMullen, p.427.
33. *Burnley Express*, 21 October 1916.
34. *Burnley Express*, 21 October 1916.

Chapter Four
1. Macdonald, p.339–40.
2. Neillands, p.292–3.
3. Neillands, p.292.
4. Gliddon, p.47.
5. Nicholson & McMullan, p.427.
6. Van Emden, p.240.
7. Brown, p.98.
8. *Blackburn Times*, 16 December 1916.
9. *Accrington Observer and Times*, 23 January 1917.
10. National Archives WO95 1294 – 2nd Division War Diary.
11. *Accrington Observer and Times*, 23 January 1917.

12. National Archives WO95 2538 – 10th Loyal North Lancs War Diary.
13. *Accrington Observer and Times*, 23 January 1917.
14. *Accrington Observer and Times*, 2 December 1916.
15. *Labour Leader*, 24 October 1914.
16. *Accrington Observer and Times*, 23 January 1917.
17. *Colne & Nelson Times*, 23 February 1917.
18. National Archives WO95 1294 – 2nd Division War Diary.
19. National Archives WO95 2538 – 10th Loyal North Lancs War Diary.
20. *Burnley News*, 29 November 1916.
21. National Archives WO95 2845 – 51st Division War Diary.
22. National Archives WO95 747 – V Corps War Diary.
23. National Archives WO95 747 – V Corps War Diary.
24. National Archives WO95 1294 – 2nd Division War Diary.
25. National Archives WO95 756 – V Corps Artillery War Diary.
26. National Archives WO95 1318 – 2nd Division Artillery War Diary.
27. National Archives WO95 1294 – 2nd Division War Diary.
28. Griffith, p.75.
29. Nicholson & McMullan, p.428.
30. National Archives WO95 747 – V Corps War Diary (The COs of 11th Border and 17th HLI reported 'friendly-fire' incidents).
31. Sheffield, p.181.
32. Chapman, p.135.
33. Nicholson & McMullan, p.429.
34. Holmes, p.115.
35. *Burnley Express*, 20 January 1917.
36. National Archives WO95 2537 – 8th East Lancs War Diary.
37. *Burnley Express*, 20 March 1917.
38. Van Emden, p.202.
39. Collinson, p.121.
40. Rawson, p.28.
41. *Burnley News*, 24 July 1918.
42. *Burnley News*, 24 July 1918.
43. *The Nelson Leader*, 23 February 1917.
44. *The Nelson Leader*, 23 March 1917.
45. IWM, Simms F.H., 11387 P462.
46. Veteran Arthur Barraclough quoted in Van Emden, p.112–3.
47. *Northwich Guardian*, 16 March 1917.

Chapter Five
1. National Archives WO95 2537 – 8th East Lancs War Diary.
2. Griffith, p.77.

3. SS 143 manual p.11.
4. National Archives WO95 2535 – 112 Brigade War Diary.
5. IWM 3476 85/1/1 Sergeant Whiteman 10th Royal Fusiliers, 37th Division.
6. Fox, p.20.
7. Nicholls, p.131.
8. *Official History of the First World War – 1917*, p.221–2.
9. *Burnley Express*, 25 April 1917.
10. *Burnley Express*, 25 April 1917.
11. Nicholls, p.142.
12. Nicholls, p.143.
13. *The War Illustrated*, 19 May 1917.
14. *The Bury Times*, 27 July 1918.
15. Nicholls, p.142.
16. Chapman, p151.
17. Fulwood Barracks Archive.
18. National Archives WO95 2513 – 37th Division War Diary.
19. *Burnley Express*, 9 May 1917.
20. Nicholls, p.22.
21. *Burnley Express*, 1 March 1919.
22. National Archives WO95 2537 – 8th East Lancs War Diary.
23. Chapman, p.165.
24. *Rossendale Free Press*, 12 May 1917.
25. Hewett. www.leedstrinity.ac.uk.
26. Norman Collins quoted in Van Emden & Humphries, p.130.
27. National Archives WO95 2298–86 Brigade War Diary.
28. National Archives WO95 2298–86 Brigade War Diary.
29. Nicholson & McMullen, p.438.
30. 163rd (Schleswig-Holstein) Regiment of the 17th Reserve Division. Quoted in Fox, p.94.
31. *Burnley News*, 14 July 1917.
32. *Burnley News*, 14 July 1917.
33. *Burnley News*, 13 June 1917.
34. National Archives WO95 2537 – 8th East Lancs War Diary.
35. British Roll of Honour.

Chapter Six

1. Riley, p.17 (handwritten narrative – Fulwood Barracks).

2. Nicholson & McMullan, p.438.
3. Van Emden, p.200.
4. Sir Douglas Haig's Despatches were published by J.M. Dent & Sons, 1919.
5. Riley, p.26 (handwritten narrative).
6. Riley, p.27 (handwritten narrative).
7. *Burnley Express*, 15 August 1917.
8. *Rossendale Free Press*, 8 August 1917.
9. Chapman, p.173.
10. National Archives WO95 2537 – 8th East Lancs War Diary.
11. Nicholson & McMullen, p.442.
12. Chapman, p.152.
13. Riley, p.23–4, 'In the Front Line 1917–18' (Unpublished 1970).
14. Riley, p.27, 'In the Front Line 1917–18' (Unpublished 1970).
15. *Burnley News*, 27 October 1917.
16. *Burnley News*, 10 October 1917.
17. *Burnley News*, 3 October 1917.
18. *Burnley Express*, 3 October 1917.
19. Riley, p.53 (handwritten narrative).
20. *Blackburn Times*, 27 October 1917.
21. nRiley, p.39, 'In the Front Line 1917–18' (Unpublished 1970).
22. Riley, p.45, 'In the Front Line 1917–18' (Unpublished 1970).
23. *Blackburn Times*, 27 October 1917.

Chapter Seven

1. Chapman, p.179.
2. Riley, p.28, 'In the Front Line 1917–18' (Unpublished 1970).
3. Chris Baker, www.1914–1918.net.
4. Riley, p.57, 'In the Front Line 1917–18' (Unpublished 1970).
5. National Archives WO95 2538 – 10th Loyal North Lancs War Diary.
6. Wylly, p.335.
7. Riley, p.80 (handwritten narrative).
8. *Burnley Express*, 19 April 1919.
9. Riley, p.16 'In the Front Line 1917–18' (Unpublished 1970).

Chapter Eight

1. National Archives WO95 2513 – 37th Division War Diary.

BIBLIOGRAPHY

Beattie, D., *Blackburn – The Development of a Lancashire Cotton Town* (Ryburn Publishing: 1992)

Beckett, I.F.W., *Haig's Generals* (Pen and Sword: 2006)

Brown, M., *Tommy Goes to War* (The History Press: 2001)

Chapman, G., *A Passionate Prodigality* (Nicholson and Watson: 1933)

Collinson, C.S., *The 11th Royal Warwicks in France* (Cornish Brothers LTD: 1928)

Crompton, G., *34 Men* (IMCC LTD: 2001)

Edgington, M.A., *Bournemouth and the First World War* (Bournemouth Local Studies: 1985)

Fox, C., *Monchy-le-Preux* (Pen and Sword: 2000)

Fuller, J.G., *Troop Morale and Popular Culture in the British and Dominion Armies 1914–18* (Clarendon: 1990)

Gliddon, G., *The Battle of the Somme- A Topographical History* (The History Press: 1998)

Griffith, P., *Battle Tactics of the Western Front* (Yale University Press: 1994)

Holding, N., *More Sources of World War I Army Ancestry* (Federation of Family History Societie: 1998)

Holmes, R., *Tommy* (HarperCollins: 2004)

Kirby, H.L., *A Visit to Foncquevillers* (THCL Books: 1985)

Macdonald, L., *Somme* (Penguin: 1983)

Neillands, R., *The First World War Generals on the Western Front 1914–18* (Robinson Publishing: 1999)

Nicholls, J., *Cheerful Sacrifice* (Leo Cooper: 1990)

Nicholson, L. & Macmullen, H.T., *History of the East Lancashire Regiment in the First World War 1914–18* (Littlebury Press: 1936)

Putkowski, J. & Sykes, J., *Shot at Dawn* (Wharncliffe Publishing: 1989)

Rawson, A., *Loos – Hill 70* (Pen and Sword: 2002)

Riley, M., 'In the Front Line' (Unpublished, 1970 – Fulwood Barracks)

Sheffield, G., *Forgotten Victory* (Headline Book Publishing: 2001)

Simkins, P., *Kitchener's Army – The Raising of the New Armies, 1914–16* (Manchester University Press: 1988)

Van Emden, R., *The Trench* (Bantam Press: 2002)

Van Emden, R. & Humphries, S., *Veterans – The Last Survivors of the First World War* (Leo Cooper: 1998)

Various, *The Golden Horseshoe* (Cassell and Co.: 1919)

Wylly, H.C., *The Loyal North Lancashire Regiment* (Royal United Services Institute: 1933)

Index

If you are interested in purchasing other books published by The History Press,
or in case you have difficulty finding any History Press books in your local bookshop,
you can also place orders directly through our website

www.thehistorypress.co.uk